PASTA

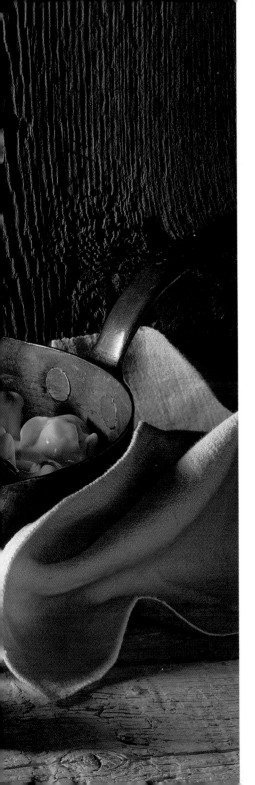

HAMLYN
new
COOKERY

PASTA

SALLY MANSFIELD

First published in Great Britain in 1994
by Hamlyn
an imprint of Reed Consumer Books Limited
Michelin House, 81 Fulham Road, London SW3 6RB
and Auckland, Melbourne, Singapore and Toronto

ISBN 0 600 58082 2

A CIP catalogue record for this book is available from the
British Library

Printed in the UK by Butler and Tanner

ACKNOWLEDGEMENTS

Art Director Jacqui Small
Art Editor Penny Stock
Designer Barbara Zuniga
Commissioning Editor Nicky Hill
Editors Jeni Fleetwood and Elsa Petersen-Schepelern
Production Controller Melanie Frantz
Photographer James Murphy
Step-by-step Photography Jonathan Lovekin
Home Economists Allyson Birch and Jane Stevenson
Stylist Jane McLeish

NOTES

Both metric and imperial measurements have been given
in all recipes. Use one set of measurements only and not a
mixture of both.

Standard level spoon measurements are used in all recipes.
1 tablespoon = one 15 ml spoon
1 teaspoon = one 5 ml spoon

Eggs should be size 3 unless otherwise stated.

Milk should be full fat unless otherwise stated.

Pepper should be freshly ground black pepper unless
otherwise stated.

Fresh herbs should be used unless otherwise stated. If
unavailable use dried herbs as an alternative but halve
the quantities stated.

Ovens should be preheated to the specified temperature
- if using a fan assisted oven, follow the manufacturer's
instructions for adjusting the time and the temperature.

Vegetarians should look for the 'V' symbol on a cheese to
ensure it is made with vegetarian rennet. There are
vegetarian forms of Parmesan, Feta, Cheddar, Cheshire,
Red Leicester, dolcelatte and many goats' cheeses,
among others.

AUTHOR'S ACKNOWLEDGEMENTS

I must say a huge thank you to Jessica Lake, who spent
hours testing and trying these recipes with me, along with
Angela, Jane, Dorcas, Di and Hillary. Of course my thanks
also go to my husband Andrew, who patiently sat through
endless dinners of pasta! (I didn't have many complaints, I
hasten to add.)

CONTENTS

INTRODUCTION

Pasta has to be the world's ultimate convenience food. It is quick and easy to prepare, absolutely delicious and extremely cheap. You can, of course, buy it fresh now, or make it yourself, but as any discerning Italian cook will tell you, dried pasta is just as good if not better.

If cooking with pasta is new to you I am sure you will find the all the recipes in this book easy to cook. The preparation time takes into account assembling the ingredients and any advance preparation such as chopping or slicing, plus any cooking which is incidental to the main cooking time, such as when sauces are cooked before a dish such as lasagne can be assembled and baked. In simpler dishes; most of the sauces will be ready by the time the pasta has cooked.

This book includes chapters on soups, sauces to serve with pasta, meat, fish, salads, and vegetarian or meat-free dishes with pasta.

Most of the recipes will serve four, but it is a simple matter to halve the recipe to serve two. When cooking for crowds, you simply double the ingredients – you won't need to make too many adjustments.

I hope you will enjoy trying my recipes and they will become firm family favourites.

COOKING PASTA

When I was first taught to cook pasta, I was told to take a strand of the cooked pasta out of the pan and hurl it against the wall. If it stuck, it was ready.

I'm not recommending you do that, although it can be a good indicator. A less messy but equally reliable test is to take a piece of pasta from the pan and squeeze it between your fingers. If it breaks cleanly, it is cooked. Test the pasta frequently and make sure you don't overcook it; sticky, soggy pasta has little to commend it.

In fact, I have suggested in most of my recipes that the dried pasta be cooked for between 8-12 minutes, but always check the packet as the brand you have bought may have different cooking times.

Fresh pasta takes much less time to cook than dried, and this kind is ready when it rises to the surface of the boiling water in which it has been cooked.

Most of the recipes in this book use dried pasta, but there is also a chapter on how to make your own. For those who have the time, and fancy having a go, it can be very satisfying, not only because it tastes good, but also because it gives you a great sense of achievement.

PASTA AND YOUR HEALTH

Until very recent times, pasta was regarded as fattening, but this is by no means true. Pasta is made up largely of carbohydrate, with virtually no fat, so you fill up quickly without the high calorie intake. It is, in fact, a high-energy food, beloved of athletes.

For an even higher fibre content, you can use wholemeal pasta. Although only a few of the recipes in this book specifically state that this type of pasta should be used, it can easily be substituted for the plain pasta. Wholemeal pasta may absorb more water during cooking, however, so do check it frequently.

HOMEMADE PASTA

'Pasta' actually means 'paste' or 'dough', and is made from durum (hard) wheat ground to a coarse semolina and mixed with water.

However, because durum wheat flour is very hard, the dough is very difficult to handle by hand, and so homemade pasta will be easier if you use a mixture of flours. Once the dough is mixed, the true artistry and skill of the accomplished pasta maker comes into play.

Pasta is not at all difficult to make yourself. Follow the directions on the right for making the dough, rolling it out with a rolling pin and cutting it to shape. (If you are very lucky, some kind friend may give you a pasta machine for your birthday!)

1 Sift the flour and salt on to a clean dry work surface, heaping the flour high around the edges to create a well in the middle. Pour the eggs, oil and liquid flavourings (if any) into the central well.

2 Using your fingers, gradually work all the dry ingredients into the egg mixture, and trying to prevent any of the liquids from spilling over the edges of the flour.

3 When all the flour has been mixed thoroughly into the liquid ingredients, knead the dough for 10 minutes, or

until it is smooth and elastic. Place the dough in a plastic bag and leave to rest for 30 minutes. This allows the gluten in the flour to become elastic.

4 Roll out the dough on to a lightly floured surface as thinly as possible without tearing it (you should be able to see through the pasta). To turn the dough, roll it lightly over the rolling in, as shown above.

5 Using a sharp knife, cut the pasta into strips to make tagliatelle, as shown above, or roll into a tube and cut crossways. You can also make many other pasta shapes – cut into big rectangular sheets for lasagne, or into squares in preparation for stuffed ravioli.

6 Homemade pasta should be left to dry for about 10 minutes before cooking. Spread it out on a clean tea towel, or hang it over an improvised 'clothes-horse' to dry.

7 When cooking fresh pasta always allow at least 1.75-3.5 litres/ 3-6 pints water to 300 g/10 oz pasta. If you have a large pasta pan, great – if not, something the size of a pressure cooker is ideal. If the worst comes to the worst, cook smaller batches in smaller pans. Give the pasta an occasional stir and partially cover the pan with a lid during the cooking time. The pasta is cooked when it rises to the top of the cooking liquid.

DRIED PASTA

This selection includes just a few of the varieties of pasta which are readily available in dried form. In general, the large shell shapes are meant to take stuffings, while hollow and ridged shapes are designed to hold as much sauce as possible.

1 SPAGHETTI (STRING LIKE):
Available in various lengths, this long tubular pasta is now made in verdi, quick-cook and wholemeal varieties.

2 FARFALLE (BUTTERFLIES):
A double-ended pasta bow with the pasta pinched together in the centre.

3 FUSILLI (CORKSCREW):
Pasta that has been twisted at the manufacturing stage.

4 TAGLIATELLE (FLAT RIBBON):
This pasta is rolled and cut into thin strips and is technically a noodle made from egg pasta.

5 PAPPARDELLE (BROAD NOODLES):
Egg noodles which are made in a similar way to tagliatelle, but cut into wider strips.

6 PENNE (QUILLS):
A tubular macaroni pasta made in various sizes, ribbed or plain.

7 CONCHIGLIE (SHELLS):
This pasta is produced in many sizes and can be ribbed or plain. Conchigliette rigate is the name given to a small ridged version.

8 CAPPELLETTI (PEAKED HATS):
As the name suggests, this pasta resembles small hats. It is made in a variety of sizes and can be either ribbed or plain.

9 ZITO COL BUCO (WIDE TUBE):
This is a wide tubular pasta, which is really only ever made plain.

10 VERMICELLI (LITTLE WORMS):
Although the literal translation of the name may be a bit off-putting, this fine pasta, often sold in little nests or clusters, is delicious with almost any kind of sauce.

11 Other forms used in this book include lumaconi (big snails), laganele, macaroni, tripolini, ruote (pasta wheels), bucato, tronchetti, spirals, twists and shells, angel hair, cannelloni and lasagne, including the convenient no-pre-cook kind. Also available are tricolore and multi-coloured pastas, and others flavoured with garlic, chilli or herbs.

However, do not be concerned if you are unable to find the precise pasta shape mentioned in the recipe's ingredients list. You simply substitute whichever kind is most easily available.

FRESH PASTA
Fresh pasta is widely available in supermarkets and delicatessens. This allows you to have all the advantages of homemade pasta without actually making it yourself.

Varieties such as tagliatelle and fettuccine are widely available, as are stuffed pastas such as tortellini and ravioli. Like homemade pasta, it cooks in just a few minutes, and is ready as soon as it rises to the surface of the boiling water.

USEFUL ITEMS OF EQUIPMENT
You don't need to go out and buy any new equipment for successful pasta results – but there are a few items which can make life a little easier in the kitchen.

THE SAUCEPAN
A truly large saucepan is ideal – preferably a straight sided stainless steel pan that can hold up to 4 litres/7 pints of liquid.

THE COLANDER
Cooked dry pasta swells to almost double its original bulk during cooking. So when it comes to straining, don't try using a small sieve. Use a large stainless steel colander – and choose one with a long handle, as the water will be boiling hot.

THE PASTA FORK
To separate cooked pasta strands, a pasta fork or spoon is really one of the essential pieces of equipment. Before I had mine I fumbled around with tongs but could never separate the pasta easily. Stainless steel is preferable, but wood is fine too.

COOKING TIPS
Pasta must be one of the easiest foods to cook, but these simple tips will help you turn out perfect pasta every time.

1 Always bring the saucepan of water to a fast rolling boil. Add a generous teaspoon or two of salt and a dash of oil. You can never season pasta satisfactorily after it has been cooked, so always salt the water before adding the pasta. The oil helps to separate the pasta and prevents the strands or shapes from sticking to each other. Always give the pasta a good stir once it has started cooking, though, as this helps to keep the pasta separate.
2 When cooking spaghetti, add it all to the pan at the same time, gently pushing the pasta into the boiling water as it softens.

3 Adjust the temperature under the pan after the pasta has been added, maintaining it at a steady boil but making sure that the water does not boil over.

4 When it comes to how much pasta you need per person, it really is up to you. I have allowed between 50-125 g/2-4 oz each. It depends upon whether the pasta will be served simply or with a substantial sauce. When in doubt it is usually better to cook less rather than more, in order to maintain the balance of pasta to sauce.

IMPORTANT INGREDIENTS

Ingredients used in this book are widely available, so you should be able to find all you need to recreate the recipes. If you do have problems for some reason, don't worry – substitute. If a recipe calls for sun-dried tomatoes and these are unobtainable, you can use fresh ripe ones with some tomato purée for extra flavour.

TOMATOES

Italy has perfect weather conditions for growing beautifully sweet, fruity, plum tomatoes. Sadly this is not always the case in England, although naturally ripened tomatoes do taste wonderful in September. I recommend you use good quality canned tomatoes instead. The canners harvest them when they are at their best, and the results can be excellent. Try out a variety of brands, as they can vary quite dramatically.

OLIVE OIL

There's no substitute for good olive oil. In my mind the best is made from the first pressing of the olives – extra virgin olive oil. It is a golden-green colour and very rich in taste, and sadly very expensive too. When cooking and serving pasta without a sauce, it is worth using the best olive oil you can buy. Some say the finest olive oils come from the South of France, but Italian, Greek and Cyprus oils are all excellent. Don't be tempted to store olive oil in the refrigerator, as it will become thick and cloudy. Keep it on the shelf out of direct sunlight, but not too near the hob, as oil will become rancid if exposed to too much heat.

ONIONS

Onions play a fundamental role in all nations' cuisines. Always choose firm ones with a pale papery skin, and avoid any that are soft or bruised. Ideally, keep onions in a cool, dark place to prevent sprouting.

Spanish onions are mild – ideal for those dishes where a delicate, rather than a robust, flavour is required.

Red-skinned onions are used in some recipes. They not only look wonderful, with their deep red layers of flesh, but also have a sweet mild flavour, which makes them perfect to eat raw in salads such as Greek Tarragon Salad (page 126).

Shallots are widely used in French cooking. They have a deep russet papery skin and look more like a garlic bulb than an onion. They have a mild yet concentrated flavour.

GARLIC

Garlic is highly favoured for its aromatic flavour and I have used it throughout the book. If you and your family prefer not to eat garlic, don't worry – it can quite easily be omitted from the recipes.

These days garlic is sold in many forms. For convenience I have used both purée and fresh cloves. Garlic purée is available in supermarkets and is usually stocked alongside the tomato purée. A general rule of thumb when using it, is to substitute about 1 teaspoon of the purée for every 2 crushed garlic cloves.

Jars of minced garlic, preserved in a little vinegar and salt, are also available. Use minced garlic very sparingly as the flavour is much more concentrated than that of garlic purée or fresh crushed garlic.

HERBS

Finding fresh herbs shouldn't be a problem, as they are now widely available all year round. Dried basil is no substitute for fresh, and this can be a bit tricky to track down during winter months. To make sure I have fresh herbs on hand, I freeze them throughout the summer. If you do need to use dried herbs, always buy the freeze-dried varieties. These have a fresher flavour and a much better texture after cooking than herbs which are dried conventionally.

HOMEMADE PASTA

Tomato Tagliatelle

250 g/8 oz strong white bread flour
½ teaspoon salt
2 eggs, beaten
1 tablespoon olive oil
2 tablespoons tomato purée
25 g/1 oz butter
250 g/8 oz mixed mushrooms, sliced if large
25 g/1 oz pecan nuts, halved
salt and pepper
small bunch of chervil, to garnish

1 Sift the flour and salt on to a clean dry work surface, heaping the flour high around the edges to create a well in the middle. Pour the beaten eggs, oil and tomato purée into the well.

2 Using your fingers, gradually work the dry ingredients into the egg mixture (trying to prevent the liquids from spilling over the edges of the flour). When all the flour has been incorporated, knead the dough for 10 minutes until smooth and elastic. Place in a plastic bag and leave to rest for 30 minutes.

3 Roll out the pasta dough on a lightly floured surface as thinly as possible without tearing it (you should be able to see through the pasta). Using a sharp knife, cut the pasta into thin strips and roll each strip into a nest. Set aside.

4 Bring at least 1.75 litres/3 pints water to the boil in a large saucepan. Add a dash of oil and a pinch of salt. Cook the pasta for 4 minutes.

5 Meanwhile, melt the butter in a saucepan and fry the mushrooms and pecan nuts for 2 minutes, stirring constantly. Add salt and pepper to taste.

6 Drain the pasta and return it to the clean pan. Add the mushroom mixture and toss well. Season to taste, and serve, garnished with chervil sprigs.

Serves 4
Preparation time: 30 minutes, plus 30 minutes resting time
Cooking time: 4 minutes

Spinach Cannelloni

PASTA:

250 g/8 oz strong white bread flour
½ teaspoon salt
2 eggs, beaten
1 tablespoon olive oil
50 g/2 oz frozen chopped spinach, thawed

FILLING:

375 g/12 oz ricotta cheese
125 g/4 oz frozen chopped spinach, thawed
1 egg, beaten
25 g/1 oz plain flour
2 tablespoons garlic purée
salt and pepper

SAUCE AND TOPPING:

1 tablespoon olive oil
1 onion, chopped
1 x 550 g/18 oz jar passata (sieved tomatoes)
2 tablespoons mixed dried herbs
250 g/8 oz mozzarella cheese, grated

1 Make the pasta. Sift the flour and salt on to a clean dry work surface, heaping the flour high around the edges to create a well in the middle. Mix the eggs, oil and spinach in a small bowl. Carefully add the mixture to the well. Gradually work the flour into the egg mixture with your fingers, (trying to prevent the liquids from spilling over the edges).

2 Once all the flour has been incorporated, knead the dough for about 10 minutes, adding a little more flour if necessary. Place the dough in a plastic bag for about 30 minutes to rest.

3 Make the filling. Mix the ricotta, spinach, egg, flour and garlic purée in a bowl. Add salt and pepper to taste. Spoon into a piping bag fitted with a large plain nozzle. Set aside.

4 Make the sauce. Heat the oil in a pan and fry the onion for 3 minutes until softened. Stir in the passata and herbs, and simmer for 5 minutes.

5 Roll out the dough on a lightly floured surface as thinly as possible without tearing it. Cut into twelve 15 x 10 cm/6 x 4 inch sheets. Bring 1.75 litres/3 pints water to the boil. Add a dash of oil and a pinch of salt. Cook the pasta, in 2 batches if necessary, for 4 minutes.

6 Remove the pasta with a slotted spoon and drain on paper towels. Pipe the filling along the width of each pasta sheet then roll them up to make filled cannelloni tubes.

7 Arrange the tubes on the base of a lightly greased 1.75 litre/3 pint rectangular ovenproof dish. Pour the sauce over and top with the grated mozzarella. Bake in a preheated oven, 190°C (375°F), Gas Mark 5, for 45 minutes.

Serves 4
Preparation time: 45 minutes, plus 30 minutes resting time
Cooking time: 45 minutes
Oven temperature: 190°C (375°F), Gas Mark 5

Beef Ravioli

Large, easy-to-handle ravioli.

PASTA:
250 g/8 oz strong white bread flour
½ teaspoon salt
2 eggs, beaten
2 tablespoons olive oil
6 tablespoons water
basil sprigs, to garnish

FILLING:
125 g/4 oz cold roast beef, minced or chopped in the food processor
125 g/4 oz fresh spinach, washed
1 onion, grated
1 garlic clove, crushed
2 tablespoons passata (sieved tomatoes)
1 egg, beaten
125 g/4 oz firm ricotta cheese, cubed
salt and pepper

1 Make the pasta dough, as described on page 7, up to step 3.

2 Make the filling. Mince the beef finely in a food processor. Cook the spinach in a saucepan with just the water that clings to the leaves after rinsing, until wilted. Drain, pressing the leaves against the colander to remove all excess liquid. Add to the beef with onion, garlic and passata. Add salt and pepper to taste and process for 30 seconds more.

4 On a lightly floured surface, roll out the dough as thinly as possible without tearing it. You should be able to see through the pasta.

5 With a crimped pastry wheel, cut twenty-four 15 x 10 cm/6 x 4 inch rectangles. Brush one-half of each rectangle with the egg and place a teaspoon of filling on each unglazed half. Place a cube of cheese on top of the filling and fold the pasta over. Seal the edges with a fork. Fill the remaining pasta rectangles in the same way. Set aside.

6 Bring at least 1.75 litres/3 pints water to the boil in a large saucepan. Add a dash of oil and a generous pinch of salt. Cook the pasta, in batches if necessary, for 4-6 minutes. Drain thoroughly, tip into a bowl and serve with plenty of black pepper, a little olive oil and a garnish of basil sprigs.

Serves 4
Preparation time: 45 minutes, plus 30 minutes resting time
Cooking time: 4-6 minutes

Gnocchi in Herb Butter

Gnocchi has to be one of the easiest forms of pasta to make, and this sauce of garlic butter and herbs is perfect.

350 g/12 oz Cyprus potatoes, peeled
1 egg yolk, beaten
125 g/4 oz plain flour
oil, see method
50 g/2 oz butter
1 teaspoon garlic purée
2 tablespoons chopped fresh parsley
salt and pepper

1 Cook the potatoes in a saucepan of boiling water for 30 minutes or until tender enough to mash. Drain well and return to the pan. Mash the potatoes, then return the pan to a low heat to allow any excess liquid to evaporate.

2 Beat in the egg yolk and flour until smooth, then turn the potato mixture out on to a floured work surface. Shape it into walnut-sized balls.

3 Flour a long pronged fork and carefully push a small ball of the paste on to the prongs. Using your second and forefinger drag the gnocchi paste up towards you. It should curl, leaving an impression on the underside. If the paste sticks, flour the fork again and don't push so hard. Dust the formed gnocchi with a little flour.

4 Bring at least 1.75 litres/3 pints water to the boil in a large saucepan. Add a dash of oil and a pinch of salt. Cook the gnocchi, in 2 batches if necessary, for 3 minutes or until they all start to float to the surface. Drain well and keep hot.

5 Melt the butter in a small frying pan and stir in the garlic purée and chopped parsley. Season to taste, and heat gently. Divide the gnocchi between 4 heated serving plates, pour over the butter mixture and toss lightly. Serve, accompanied by a bowl of grated Parmesan cheese.

Serves 4
Preparation time: 45 minutes
Cooking time: 3-6 minutes

No Fuss Lasagne

This recipe is called 'no fuss lasagne' because it does not require special pasta-making equipment or complicated cooking arrangements. While the pasta dough is resting, you can save time by getting on with making the meat filling and the cheese sauce.

PASTA:

200 g/7 oz strong white bread flour
½ teaspoon salt
2 eggs, beaten
1 tablespoon olive oil

FILLING:

1 tablespoon olive oil
1 onion, chopped finely
1 tablespoon garlic purée
375 g/12 oz lean minced beef
4 tablespoons tomato purée
1 x 397 g/14 oz can plum tomatoes
1 beef stock cube, crumbled
2 tablespoons mixed dried herbs

SAUCE:

40 g/1½ oz butter
40 g/1½ oz plain flour
450 ml/¾ pint milk
250 g/8 oz Cheddar cheese or Pecorino
  cheese, grated
salt and pepper

1 Make the pasta as described on page 7, up to step 3. Leave to rest.
2 Meanwhile, make the filling. Heat the oil in a saucepan and add the onion. Stir in the garlic purée. Fry for 3 minutes until the onion is softened. Add the remaining filling ingredients, stir well and simmer uncovered for 35 minutes until the mixture has thickened and reduced slightly.
3 Make the sauce. Melt the butter in a saucepan. Stir in the flour and cook for 1 minute. Add the milk gradually, whisking or beating the sauce over moderate heat until thickened. Season to taste. Beat in half the cheese, then cover the sauce closely and set aside.

4 On a lightly floured surface, roll out the pasta as thinly as possible without breaking it (you should be able to see through the pasta). Cut it into 8 sheets, each 16 x 10 cm/ 6½ x 4 inches.
5 Bring at least 1.75 litres/3 pints water to the boil in a large saucepan. Add a dash of oil and a generous pinch of salt. Cook the lasagne sheets, in 2 batches if necessary, for 2 minutes.
6 Remove the pasta with a slotted spoon; drain on paper towels. Lay 2 sheets in the base of a lightly greased 1.75 litre/3 pint ovenproof dish. Spoon over one-third of the mince filling followed by one-third of the sauce. Continue layering the ingredients in this manner, using 3 sheets of lasagne for each of the following pasta layers, finishing with cheese sauce. Scatter the remaining cheese on top.
7 Bake in a preheated oven, 190°C (375°F), Gas Mark 5, for about 35-45 minutes until golden.

Serves 4
Preparation time: 45 minutes, plus 30 minutes resting time
Cooking time: 45 minutes
Oven temperature: 190°C (375°F), Gas Mark 5

Tomato Conchigliette Rigate

1 tablespoon olive oil
1 onion, chopped finely
1 teaspoon ground cumin
1 kg/2 lb plum tomatoes, peeled and chopped or
2 x 397 g/14 oz cans chopped tomatoes
2 tablespoons tomato purée
1 teaspoon caster sugar
1.2 litres/2 pints hot chicken stock
125 g/4 oz dried conchigliette rigate or other small pasta shapes
salt and pepper
a few basil leaves, torn

1 Heat the oil in a large saucepan, add the onion and fry for 3 minutes, stirring constantly until softened but not browned. Stir in the cumin and fry for about 1 minute more.

2 Stir in the tomatoes, tomato purée and sugar. Simmer the mixture, covered, for 5 minutes.

3 Gradually add the stock. Bring to the boil, add the dried pasta and stir in salt and pepper to taste. Lower the heat and simmer for 15 minutes. Just before serving, stir in the torn basil leaves. Serve with crusty bread.

Serves 4
Preparation time: 15 minutes
Cooking time: about 28 minutes

1 Melt the butter in the oil in a large pan. Add the onion rings and fry for 5 minutes until softened and lightly browned. Reduce the heat and sprinkle the sugar over the onions. Stir until dissolved. Raise the heat and fry the onions until golden and caramelized.

2 Stir in the tomato purée and flour. Cook, stirring constantly, for 1 minute, then gradually stir in the stock. Bring to the boil.

3 Add the noodles or the pasta spirals, lower the heat and simmer for 6-12 minutes. Meanwhile, toast one side of each baguette slice under a hot grill. Rub the cut surface of the garlic over each untoasted side, top with a slice of mozzarella, then return to the grill for 3 minutes until the cheese bubbles. Serve the soup in heated bowls with the mozzarella toast.

Serves 4
Preparation time: 15 minutes
Cooking time: 23 minutes

French Onion Soup with Noodles

25 g/1 oz butter
2 tablespoons olive oil
1 kg/2 lb large Spanish onions, sliced
1 teaspoon demerara sugar
½ tablespoon tomato purée
1 tablespoon plain flour
1.2 litres/2 pints hot vegetable or chicken stock
125 g/4 oz dried noodles, broken into short lengths, or pasta spirals
1 small French baguette, sliced into wedges
1 garlic clove, halved
125 g/4 oz mozzarella cheese, sliced

Winter Broth

1 tablespoon olive oil
1 large shallot, chopped finely
250 g/8 oz mixed vegetables,
    such as potatoes, carrots and leeks,
    chopped finely
2 tablespoons mixed dried herbs
125 g/4 oz lean minced beef
4 tablespoons tomato purée
1 tablespoon yeast extract
1 tablespoon Worcestershire sauce
1.2 litres/2 pints hot beef stock
75 g/3 oz dried pipe bucato
    or macaroni
25 g/1 oz Cheddar cheese, grated
salt and pepper

1 Heat the olive oil in a large saucepan. Add the chopped shallot and mixed vegetables with the mixed dried herbs. Fry, stirring constantly for 5 minutes until the vegetables are softened and lightly browned.
2 Stir in the beef and fry for a further 15 minutes, stirring occasionally until the meat has browned.
3 Add the tomato purée, the yeast extract and Worcestershire sauce, stir well and cook over low heat for about 2 minutes.
4 Gradually add the stock and bring to the boil. Add the pasta, with salt and pepper to taste. Lower the heat and simmer for 20 minutes. Serve, sprinkled with the grated cheese.

Serves 4-6
Preparation time: 20 minutes
Cooking time: 42 minutes

Country Vegetable Soup

1 tablespoon vegetable oil	1 leek, sliced finely
25 g/1 oz butter	1.2 litres/2 pints hot vegetable stock
1 onion, chopped	75 g/3 oz dried spaghetti
2 carrots, chopped finely	2 tablespoons chopped mixed
1 potato, chopped finely	fresh herbs
1 parsnip, chopped finely	salt and pepper
¼ swede, diced finely	

1 Heat the oil in a large saucepan with the butter. Once the mixture is sizzling add the vegetables and fry them over gentle heat for 8 minutes or until soft, stirring occasionally.

2 Add the stock and bring to the boil. Wrap the spaghetti in a clean dry tea towel. Holding both ends of the towel, pull it towards you over the end of the table, breaking the spaghetti into 2.5 cm/1 inch lengths. Add to the saucepan, lower the heat and simmer for 8 minutes. Stir in salt and pepper to taste, sprinkle over the herbs and serve.

Serves 4
Preparation time: 15 minutes
Cooking time: 16 minutes

VARIATIONS

Beefy Vegetable Soup

Heat the oil and butter as in the main recipe and add 125 g/4 oz sliced cooked beef with the vegetables. Proceed as in the main recipe, stirring in 2 tablespoons tomato purée after adding the spaghetti.

Prawn and Vegetable Soup

Heat the oil and butter as in the main recipe. Add 125 g/4 oz broccoli florets with the other vegetables. Continue as in the main recipe, adding 125 g/4 oz peeled, cooked prawns 3 minutes before the end of the cooking time.

Hot and Sour Soup

Look out for chilli oil in Chinese supermarkets. This fiery hot liquid is the authentic seasoning for Hot and Sour Soup. You can replace the red chillies with 1 tablespoon of the oil.

1 tablespoon olive oil
125 g/4 oz dried egg thread noodles
4 spring onions, sliced diagonally
1 tablespoon garlic purée
1 x 2.5 cm/1 inch piece fresh root
    ginger, peeled and chopped finely
    or crushed
2 red chillies, deseeded and
    chopped finely
125 g/4 oz chestnut or brown cap
    mushrooms, sliced
125 g/4 oz cooked chicken
    breast, shredded
1 carrot, cut into small thin sticks
900 ml/1½ pints hot chicken stock,
    preferably Chinese-style
1 egg, beaten
finely chopped spring onions,
    to garnish

1 Bring at least 1.75 litres/3 pints water to the boil in a large saucepan. Add a dash of oil and a generous pinch of salt. Add the pasta, cover the pan and remove it from the heat. Set the pasta aside, in the pan, for 6 minutes.
2 Meanwhile, heat the remaining oil in a large saucepan. Fry the spring onions for about 2 minutes, stirring constantly. Add the garlic purée, ginger and chillies.
3 Stir in the mushrooms, chicken and carrot, with the stock. Bring to the boil, lower the heat and simmer for 5 minutes.
4 Drain the thread noodles, snip them into short lengths and add to the simmering soup.

5 Add the beaten egg a little at a time, stirring well between each addition. As soon as the egg is cooked, serve the soup in heated bowls, garnished with chopped spring onions.

Serves 4
Preparation time: 15 minutes
Cooking time: about 10 minutes

Pasta and Chickpea Soup

2 tablespoons olive oil
2 garlic cloves, crushed
1 teaspoon ground cumin
1 onion, chopped finely
1 celery stick, chopped finely
2 tablespoons tomato purée
2 tablespoons ready-made pesto
1 x 397 g/14 oz can chopped
  tomatoes with herbs
1 x 432 g/14½ oz can chickpeas,
  drained
50 g/2 oz drained sweetcorn niblets
900 ml/1½ pints hot vegetable or
  chicken stock
75 g/3 oz tiny dried pasta shapes
salt and pepper
1 tablespoon chopped fresh parsley,
  to garnish

1 Heat the oil in a saucepan and fry the garlic, cumin, onion, and celery for 3 minutes, stirring constantly until the vegetables have softened.
2 Stir in the tomato purée and the pesto. Cook for about 1 minute, then add the tomatoes, chickpeas, sweetcorn and stock, with salt and pepper to taste. Bring to the boil, add the pasta, lower the heat and simmer for 6-8 minutes or until the pasta is just tender. Serve at once, in heated bowls.

Serves 4
Preparation time: 10 minutes
Cooking time: 10-12 minutes

Red Lentil and Pastini Soup

125 g/4 oz red lentils
1 tablespoon vegetable oil
1 onion, chopped
2 garlic cloves, crushed
1 carrot, diced
2 celery sticks, sliced
1.2 litres /2 pints hot beef stock

300 ml/½ pint passata
  (sieved tomatoes)
50 g/2 oz dried pastini
4 tablespoons natural yogurt or
  crème fraîche
25 g/1 oz Parmesan cheese, grated
salt and pepper

1 Par-cook the lentils in a saucepan of boiling water for 10 minutes. Drain and set aside. Heat the oil in a large saucepan, and fry the onion and garlic for about 3 minutes.

2 Add the drained lentils to the pan with the carrot and celery. Fry for 3 minutes more, or until the onion is softened.

3 Stir in the stock and passata, with salt and pepper to taste. Simmer, covered, for 30 minutes. Add the pasta and simmer for a further 10 minutes.

4 Off the heat, stir in the yogurt or crème fraîche. Pour the soup into a tureen, sprinkle over the Parmesan cheese and serve.

Serves 4
Preparation time: 15 minutes
Cooking time: about 1 hour

Clam and Sweetcorn Chowder

175 g/6 oz fresh clams, cleaned, or
2 x 290 g/9½ oz cans baby clams
in brine, drained
1 tablespoon olive oil
1 onion, chopped finely
1 teaspoon ground turmeric

1 teaspoon plain flour
50 g/2 oz drained canned
sweetcorn niblets
900 ml/1½ pints hot vegetable or
fish stock
50 g/2 oz dried vermicelli
4 tablespoons double cream
salt and pepper
TO GARNISH:
1 tablespoon chopped fresh parsley
a few sprigs of flat leaf
parsley

1 If using fresh clams put them in a large saucepan with 2 tablespoons of water. Cover with a lid and cook for 8 minutes or until the shells have opened. Discard any clams with shells which remain shut. Drain the rest of the clams, and remove them from their shells. Set aside.

2 Heat the oil in a large saucepan, add the onion and fry for 5 minutes or until softened. Stir in the turmeric and fry for 1 minute more.

3 Stir in the flour and fry for about 1 minute, then remove the pan from the heat.

4 Add the fresh or drained canned clams to the onion mixture with the sweetcorn, hot stock and pasta. Simmer for 8 minutes. Add salt and pepper to taste and stir in the double cream. Serve in heated bowls, sprinkled with chopped fresh parsley and garnished with sprigs of flat leaf parsley.

Serves 4
Preparation time: 20 minutes
Cooking time: 23 minutes

Country Bean and Pasta Broth

75 g/3 oz country bean mix or
    25 g/1 oz each dried kidney beans,
    pinto beans and black-eyed beans
25 g/1 oz dried porcini mushrooms
1 tablespoon olive oil
2 shallots, chopped finely
2 garlic cloves, crushed
125 g/4 oz button mushrooms, diced
2 tablespoons chopped mixed
    fresh herbs
50 g/2 oz mini dried pasta shapes
1.2 litres/2 pints hot beef stock
salt and pepper
chopped fresh herbs, to garnish

1 Soak the beans overnight in cold water in a covered bowl.

2 The next day, drain the beans and place them in a large saucepan with water to cover. Bring to the boil and boil vigorously for 10 minutes. Skim any scum off the surface of the liquid and reduce the heat. Simmer, covered, for 1 hour, or until all the beans are very tender.

3 Place the dried mushrooms in a bowl, cover with boiling water and set aside for 15 minutes, then drain, and reserve the liquid.

4 Heat the oil in a large saucepan and fry the shallots and garlic for 3 minutes. Add the mushrooms; stir well. Add the herbs and pasta shapes. Drain the beans and add them to the saucepan with the hot stock, reserved mushroom liquid and

salt and pepper to taste. Bring to the boil, lower the heat and simmer for about 12 minutes. Serve at once, sprinkled with chopped, mixed fresh herbs, to garnish.

Serves 4
Preparation time: 10 minutes plus overnight soaking
Cooking time: about 1¼ hours

Beef and Pasta Soup

1 tablespoon olive oil
1 onion, sliced
2 carrots, chopped
250 g/8 oz sirloin steak, finely diced
2 tablespoons tomato purée
1 tablespoon Worcestershire sauce
2 bay leaves
1 bouquet garni

1.2 litres/2 pints hot beef stock
3 tablespoons dry sherry
50 g/2 oz tiny dried star pasta shapes
salt and pepper

TO GARNISH:
1 tablespoon chopped fresh thyme
a few sage leaves

1 Heat the oil in a large saucepan and fry the onion, carrots and diced beef for about 3 minutes. Stir in the tomato purée and Worcestershire sauce. Add the bay leaves, bouquet garni, stock and sherry. Simmer, covered, for 1 hour. Stir in salt and pepper to taste.

2 Bring the soup to the boil, add the pasta and cook for 6-8 minutes or until just tender. Check the seasoning. Remove the bay leaves and bouquet garni. Serve in heated bowls, garnished with fresh thyme and sage leaves.

Serves 4
Preparation time: 20 minutes
Cooking time: about 1¼ hours

VARIATIONS

Chicken and Sweetcorn Soup

Omit the beef in the main recipe, replacing it with 300 g/10 oz skinned chicken breast cut into fine strips. Substitute chicken stock for the beef stock and add 50 g/2 oz drained canned sweetcorn niblets with the pasta. Proceed as for the main recipe.

Prawn and Spring Onion Soup

Substitute fish stock for the chicken stock. Omit the beef. Simmer the soup for 30 minutes instead of 1 hour after adding the vegetables. Finally add 300 g/10 oz peeled cooked prawns when the pasta is almost tender. Simmer for 2 minutes and serve. Garnish with diced spring onion instead of the thyme and sage recommended in the main recipe.

Pesto Tortellini Soup

1 tablespoon olive oil
175 g/6 oz dried tortellini
2 garlic cloves, crushed
1 onion, chopped finely
1 bunch of basil, chopped
250 ml/8 fl oz coconut milk
250 ml/8 fl oz milk
2 tablespoons grated
    Parmesan cheese
salt

1 Bring at least 1.75 litres/3 pints water to the boil in a large saucepan. Add a dash of oil and a generous pinch of salt. Add the pasta, lower the heat and simmer for 8-12 minutes or until just tender.
2 Meanwhile, heat the remaining olive oil in a saucepan, add the garlic and onion and fry over gentle heat until softened.
3 Set aside 2 tablespoons of the chopped basil for the garnish. Add the remaining basil to the pan with the coconut milk and milk. Simmer

for 1 minute. Drain the pasta and add it to the soup. Simmer for 1 minute more, then sprinkle over the Parmesan cheese. Serve the soup in heated bowls, garnished with the reserved basil.

Serves 4
Preparation time: 10 minutes
Cooking time: 15 minutes

Quick-cook Macaroni and Mussel Soup

Farmed fresh mussels are now available almost all the year; but for the best flavour buy them during their season, which is from September to April.

oil, see method
75 g/3 oz quick-cook dried macaroni
500 g/1 lb fresh mussels, scrubbed and bearded
250 ml/8 fl oz red wine
1 teaspoon garlic purée
4 tablespoons chopped mixed fresh herbs
1 x 397 g/14 oz can chopped tomatoes
450 ml/¾ pint hot fish stock
salt and pepper
sprigs of fresh herbs, to garnish

1 Bring 1.75 litres/3 pints water to the boil in a large saucepan. Add a dash of oil and a generous pinch of salt. Add the pasta and cook for 8-12 minutes, until just tender.
2 Meanwhile, check over the mussels. Discard any open shells which do not close immediately when tapped on the work surface. Place the mussels in a large saucepan with the wine, garlic purée and 2 tablespoons of the herbs. Cover and simmer for 5 minutes or until all the shells have opened. Discard any that remain shut.

3 Drain the mussel cooking liquid into a clean saucepan. Either leave the cooked mussels whole, or remove them from their shells. Add them to the liquid in the pan with the tomatoes and fish stock. Drain the macaroni and add it to the mussel mixture with the remaining herbs.

4 Simmer the soup for 5 minutes, add salt and pepper to taste and serve at once, garnished with the sprigs of fresh herbs.

Serves 4
Preparation time: 20 minutes
Cooking time: 17 minutes

Onion Tripolini Soup

2 tablespoons olive oil
1-2 Spanish onions, sliced into rings
5 garlic cloves, crushed
1 tablespoon demerara sugar
1.2 litres/2 pints hot vegetable stock
50 g/2 oz dried tripolini

4 thickly-cut slices fresh farmhouse
  bread, cubed
salt and pepper
1 tablespoon chopped fresh parsley,
  to garnish

1 Heat the oil in a large saucepan. Add the onions and garlic and fry for about 5 minutes until softened. Sprinkle the sugar over the onions and continue to fry over a moderate heat until the onions have caramelized.
2 Stir in the stock. Bring to the boil, lower the heat and simmer for 5 minutes. Add salt and pepper to taste.
3 Add the pasta to the stock; simmer for 8 minutes more. Pour the soup into a large tureen and stir in the cubed bread. Scatter the chopped parsley on top and serve immediately.

Serves 4
Preparation time: 15 minutes
Cooking time: 18 minutes

Olive Oil, Chilli and Garlic Spaghetti

This type of dried pasta hasn't been available for very long. When you first remove it from the packet, the pasta smells as though it is going to taste quite garlicky, but it is the chilli flavour that really comes through when cooked.

6 tablespoons olive oil
500 g/1 lb chilli and garlic spaghetti
1 teaspoon black pepper
1 x 285 g/9½ oz jar antipasto pepperoni condiverdi
2 tablespoons chopped fresh parsley
125 g/4 oz Parmesan cheese, in one piece
salt and pepper

1 Bring at least 1.75 litres/3 pints water to the boil in a large saucepan. Add a dash of oil and a generous pinch of salt. Cook the pasta for about 8-12 minutes, until just tender.

2 Drain the pasta and return it to the clean pan. Add the black pepper, remaining olive oil, antipasto and parsley, with salt and pepper to taste. Stir well. Simmer for about 1 minute or until thoroughly heated through.

3 Spoon the pasta on to heated plates. Using a potato peeler, pare shavings of Parmesan cheese over the pasta. Serve at once.

Serves 4
Preparation time: 10 minutes
Cooking time: 13 minutes

Rich Plum Tomato Sauce with Spaghetti

For the true flavour of this sauce to develop, it is best to use those red plum tomatoes that have ripened slowly and naturally in the sun – when cooked with a pinch of sugar, add a depth of sweetness to the overall flavour.

oil, see method
375 g/12 oz dried spaghetti
SAUCE:
1 tablespoon olive oil
1 onion, chopped finely
2 garlic cloves, crushed
125 g/4 oz button mushrooms, chopped finely
2 carrots, chopped finely
750 g/1½ lb fresh plum tomatoes
2 tablespoons tomato purée
¼ teaspoon sugar
4 tablespoons single cream
salt and pepper
TO GARNISH:
grated Parmesan cheese
1 tablespoon oregano leaves

1 Make the sauce. Heat the oil in a large saucepan. Add the onion, garlic, mushrooms and carrots, and fry over moderate heat for 5 minutes or until softened.
2 Meanwhile, fill a large saucepan with water, and bring to the boil. Make a cross at the base of each tomato and plunge them into the water for 30 seconds. Remove the tomatoes with a slotted spoon and plunge them into cold water. Drain, and peel off the skins.
3 Chop the tomatoes and add them to the onion mixture with the tomato purée and sugar. Stir well. Cover the pan and simmer the sauce for 20 minutes, stirring occasionally. Add salt and pepper to taste.
4 Fifteen minutes before the end of the cooking time, bring at least 1.75 litres/3 pints water to the boil in a large saucepan. Add a dash of oil and a pinch of salt. Cook the pasta for 8-12 minutes, until just tender. Drain the pasta, pile it into a heated bowl and drizzle over a little extra oil if you wish. Season with freshly ground black pepper.
5 Stir the cream into the tomato sauce, spoon over the pasta and sprinkle with grated Parmesan cheese and oregano. Serve at once.

Serves 4
Preparation time: 20 minutes
Cooking time: 26 minutes

Herb and Garlic Tronchetti

oil, see method

375 g/12 oz dried egg tronchetti

SAUCE:

2 tablespoons olive oil

1 onion, finely chopped

4 garlic cloves, crushed

**2 red peppers, cored, deseeded and
  sliced finely**

1 tablespoon chopped fresh basil

1 tablespoon chopped fresh oregano

1 tablespoon chopped fresh parsley

300 ml/½ pint double cream

salt and pepper

TO GARNISH:

1 tablespoon torn mixed fresh herbs

shavings of Parmesan cheese (optional)

1 Bring at least 1.75 litres/3 pints water to the boil in a large saucepan. Add a dash of oil and a generous pinch of salt. Cook the pasta for about 8-12 minutes, until just tender.

2 Meanwhile, make the sauce. Heat the olive oil in a large frying pan. Add the chopped onion, the crushed garlic and the finely sliced red peppers, and then add salt and pepper to taste. Fry the mixture over a moderate heat for about 3-5 minutes until the onions are softened, but not browned.

3 Sprinkle over the chopped basil, oregano and parsley, stir in the cream and simmer the sauce for about 1 minute more.

4 Drain the pasta and add it to the herb and pepper sauce. Stir well, tip into a heated bowl and serve, garnished with the fresh herbs. Shavings of Parmesan cheese may be pared over before serving if liked.

Serves 4
Preparation time: 15 minutes
Cooking time: 12 minutes

Farfalle alla Napoletana

2 tablespoons olive oil
1 onion, chopped
2 garlic cloves, crushed
2 carrots, chopped finely, blanched
2 red peppers, cored, deseeded and
    chopped finely
4 large tomatoes, chopped

150 ml/¼ pint red wine
1 x 397 g/14 oz can chopped
    tomatoes with herbs
375 g/12 oz dried farfalle
salt and pepper
1 bunch of basil for garnish

1 Heat the oil in a large frying pan. Add the chopped onion and garlic and fry for about 3 minutes until softened but not coloured.

2 Add the carrots and red peppers and fry for a further 3 minutes. Stir in the chopped fresh tomatoes with the red wine and canned tomatoes. Add salt and pepper to taste. Simmer, partially covered, for 15 minutes.

3 Meanwhile, bring at least 1.75 litres/3 pints water to the boil in a large saucepan. Add a dash of oil and a generous pinch of salt. Cook the pasta for about 8-12 minutes, until just tender.

4 Drain the pasta, tip it on to a heated large serving platter, and season with black pepper. Drizzle with a little more oil if you wish. Pour over the sauce. Shred the basil leaves and scatter them over the sauce to garnish.

Serves 4
Preparation time: 15 minutes
Cooking time: 21 minutes

VARIATIONS

Bacon and Sweetcorn Farfalle

Make the sauce, as for the main recipe. Five minutes before the end of the cooking time add about 125 g/4 oz grilled rindless back bacon rashers, crumbled, with 125 g/4 oz sliced button mushrooms and 50 g/2 oz drained canned sweetcorn niblets. Serve the sauce over the cooked pasta as in the main recipe.

Coriander and Sun-dried Tomato Farfalle

Make the sauce as for the main recipe, omitting the carrots and basil. Substitute 8 sliced, sun-dried tomatoes and 4 tablespoons chopped coriander leaves scattered over the sauce to garnish.

Spaghetti Carbonara

Many carbonara sauces are creamy, having been finished with lashings of double cream. There is no cream included in this recipe but the eggs added at the end will give it a truly creamy flavour.

1 tablespoon olive oil
375 g/12 oz dried spaghetti
25 g/1 oz butter
1 onion, chopped
375 g/12 oz rindless smoked back bacon, chopped
4 eggs, beaten
75 g/3 oz Parmesan cheese, grated
125 g/4 oz Pecorino cheese, grated
1 tablespoon chopped fresh parsley, to garnish

1 Bring at least 1.75 litres/3 pints water to the boil in a large saucepan. Add a dash of oil and a generous pinch of salt. Cook the spaghetti for about 8-12 minutes, until just tender.

2 Meanwhile heat the remaining oil and butter in a very large frying pan. Fry the onion and bacon pieces until crisp. Remove from the heat.

3 Drain the pasta. Pour a little of the oil from the bacon mixture into the clean pasta pan. Return the pasta to the pan and stir over moderate heat for 1 minute. Add the bacon mixture and toss well. Make a slight dip in the centre and add the eggs, tossing the pasta constantly over the heat for 2 minutes or until the eggs have just cooked.

4 Set aside one-third of the grated Parmesan cheese. Add the rest, with the Pecorino cheese, to the pasta. Spoon the pasta on to heated plates, sprinkle with the reserved Parmesan and garnish with the chopped parsley.

Serves 4
Preparation time: 20 minutes
Cooking time: 15 minutes

Walnut Orecchiette with Camembert and Gruyère

4 tablespoons olive oil
300 g/10 oz dried orecchiette
2 garlic cloves, crushed
125 g/4 oz walnut pieces
2 plum tomatoes, cut into wedges
50 g/2 oz Camembert cheese
50 g/2 oz Gruyère cheese
1 bunch of chives, snipped
salt

1 Bring at least 1.75 litres/3 pints water to the boil in a large saucepan. Add a dash of oil and generous a pinch of salt. Cook the pasta for about 8-12 minutes, until just tender.
2 Drain the pasta, then set it aside. Heat the remaining oil in a large saucepan, add the garlic, walnuts and tomatoes and fry for 1 minute, stirring. Add the drained pasta to the walnut sauce and toss well. Reduce the heat.
3 Cut the Camembert into chunks, and grate the Gruyère. Add both cheeses to the sauce, followed by all except 2 tablespoons of the

snipped chives. Toss well, spoon on to heated plates and garnish with the remaining chives.

Serves 4
Preparation time: 10 minutes
Cooking time: 15 minutes

Sweet Spicy Aubergine Sauce

2 tablespoons olive oil

300 g/10 oz dried penne rigate

1 teaspoon sesame or poppy seeds

1 onion, chopped finely

1 red pepper, cored, deseeded
   and chopped

250 g/8 oz aubergines, chopped

½ red chilli, deseeded and chopped

2 tablespoons tomato purée

50 ml/2 fl oz water

1 tablespoon cider vinegar

2 tablespoons chopped fresh coriander

salt and pepper

1 Bring at least 1.75 litres/3 pints water to the boil in a large saucepan. Add a dash of oil and a pinch of salt. Cook the pasta for 8-12 minutes, until just tender.
2 Meanwhile, heat the remaining oil in a large saucepan. Add the sesame or poppy seeds with the onion. Fry for 2 minutes, then add the red pepper, aubergines and chilli, and fry for 5 minutes, stirring constantly.
3 Stir in the tomato purée, measured water and vinegar. Add salt and pepper to taste and simmer for 10 minutes.
4 Drain the pasta and return it to the clean pan. Add the aubergine mixture and toss well. Stir in the coriander and serve, with ciabbata bread, if liked.

Serves 4
Preparation time: 10-15 minutes
Cooking time: 18 minutes

Pesto Fusilli

1 tablespoon olive oil
375 g/12 oz dried fusilli
2 garlic cloves, crushed
4 tablespoons finely chopped
fresh basil
2 tablespoons grated Parmesan
cheese
25 g/1 oz pine nuts, toasted and
chopped finely
150 ml/¼ pint double cream or
crème fraîche
salt and pepper

TO GARNISH:
a few basil leaves
shavings of Parmesan cheese

1 Bring at least 1.75 litres/3 pints water to the boil in a large saucepan. Add a dash of oil and a generous pinch of salt. Cook the pasta for about 8-12 minutes, until just tender.
2 Meanwhile, heat the remaining oil in a small saucepan. Fry the crushed garlic for about 2 minutes, then stir in the basil, Parmesan cheese and pine nuts. Fry the mixture over a low heat, stirring constantly, for about 1 minute. Stir in the cream or crème fraîche, and add salt and freshly ground black pepper to taste.
3 Drain the pasta, return it to the clean pan and add the sauce. Stir well. Garnish with basil, a few shavings of Parmesan and plenty of black pepper.

Serves 4
Preparation time: 10 minutes
Cooking time: 12 minutes

Mushroom Gruyère Melt

25 g/1 oz butter
250 g/8 oz button mushrooms, finely chopped
125 g/4 oz chanterelle mushrooms, finely chopped
2 garlic cloves, crushed
oil, see method
300 g/10 oz fresh tortellini
4 tablespoons double cream
flat leaf parsley, to garnish
SAUCE:
25 g/1 oz butter
25 g/1 oz plain flour
450 ml/¾ pint milk
75 g/3 oz Gruyère cheese, grated
salt and pepper

1 Make the sauce. Melt the butter in a saucepan. Add the flour and cook for 1 minute. Add the milk gradually, whisking or beating the sauce over moderate heat until thickened. Stir in the Gruyère cheese, with salt and pepper to taste. Set aside.
2 Melt the butter in a large saucepan; add the mushrooms and garlic, with salt and pepper to taste. Fry over low heat for 5 minutes until the mushrooms have cooked down. Remove from the heat.
3 Bring at least 1.75 litres/3 pints water to the boil in a large saucepan. Add a dash of oil and a generous pinch of salt. Cook the pasta for 4-6 minutes, or until it rises to the surface of the boiling water.

4 Meanwhile, add the Gruyère sauce to the mushroom mixture. Stir in the cream and cook gently over low heat for about 2 minutes until thoroughly heated through.
5 Drain the pasta and add to the sauce. Toss well to mix, and check the seasoning. Serve at once, garnished with flat leaf parsley.

Serves 4
Preparation time: 20 minutes
Cooking time: 16 minutes

Chilli Balsamic Tagliatelle

4 tablespoons olive oil
375 g/12 oz fresh tagliatelle
2 garlic cloves, crushed
2 red chillies, deseeded and chopped
4 tablespoons balsamic vinegar
2 tablespoons orange juice

3 tablespoons ready-made red pesto
1 bunch of spring onions, shredded
25 g/1 oz toasted hazelnuts, chopped
salt
2 tablespoons chopped mixed fresh
    herbs, to garnish

1 Bring at least 1.75 litres/3 pints water to the boil in a large saucepan. Add a dash of oil and a pinch of salt. Cook the pasta for 4-6 minutes or until it rises to the surface of the boiling water.
2 Meanwhile, heat the remaining oil in a saucepan. Add the garlic and chillies and fry for 2 minutes. Reduce the heat and stir in the remaining ingredients.
3 Drain the pasta and add it to the garlic and chilli dressing, tossing well. Serve at once, garnished with the herbs.

Serves 4
Preparation time: 10 minutes
Cooking time: 6 minutes

VARIATIONS

Mushrooms and Black Olive Tagliatelle

Cook the pasta as in the main recipe. Add 50 g/2 oz sliced button mushrooms and 50 g/2 oz halved black olives when frying the garlic and chillies, and continue as for the main recipe.

Raspberry and Thyme Tagliatelle

Cook the pasta as in the main recipe. When making the sauce omit the balsamic vinegar and replace it with 4 tablespoons raspberry vinegar, then add 2 tablespoons chopped fresh thyme with the pesto and continue as in the main recipe.

Red Pesto with Spaghetti Verdi

Plain spaghetti can be used in this recipe, but the colour of the spinach-flavoured variety makes it the perfect foil for the red pesto sauce.

2 tablespoons olive oil
375 g/12 oz spaghetti verdi
3 garlic cloves, crushed
6 tablespoons ready-made red pesto
3 tablespoons orange juice or
   balsamic vinegar
salt and pepper

1 Bring at least 1.75 litres/3 pints water to the boil in a large saucepan. Add a dash of oil and a generous pinch of salt. Cook the pasta for about 8-12 minutes, until just tender.
2 Three minutes before the end of the cooking time, heat the remaining oil in a large frying pan. Add the garlic and fry for 2 minutes. Reduce the heat and stir in the pesto and orange juice or balsamic vinegar, and add salt and pepper to taste. Simmer for about 1 minute.
3 Drain the pasta and add it to the sauce. Toss well, sprinkle with more black pepper and serve at once.

Serves 4
Preparation time: 7 minutes
Cooking time: 8-12 minutes

Wholemeal Fusilli with Spinach Cheese Sauce

Wholemeal pasta contains more fibre, and has a wonderfully nutty taste. You can substitute it for plain pasta in most of the recipes in this book.

1 tablespoon olive oil
300 g/10 oz fresh wholemeal fusilli, or other short, ridged pasta, or plain pasta
250 g/8 oz fresh spinach, washed
2 garlic cloves, crushed
¼ teaspoon grated nutmeg
300 ml/½ pint single cream
250 g/8 oz mascarpone cheese
salt and pepper
toasted flaked almonds, to garnish

1 Bring at least 1.75 litres/3 pints water to the boil in a large saucepan. Add a dash of oil and a generous pinch of salt. Cook the pasta for 4-6 minutes, or until it rises to the surface of the boiling water.

2 Meanwhile, wash the spinach leaves and discard any tough stalks. Place the leaves in a large saucepan with just the water that clings to the leaves. Cook for 5 minutes or until the leaves have wilted.

3 Remove from the heat, drain the spinach well and squeeze it between 2 plates to remove all the excess water. Chop the spinach finely and set it aside.

4 Heat the remaining oil in a large saucepan and fry the garlic over a low heat for 2 minutes until softened. Stir in the nutmeg, the cream and the mascarpone cheese. Add salt and pepper to taste, raise the heat and bring to just below boiling point. Add the spinach, stir and cook for about 1 minute.

5 Drain the pasta and add to the spinach sauce. Toss well, and season again if necessary. Serve at once, garnished with toasted flaked almonds.

Serves 4
Preparation time: 20 minutes
Cooking time: 9 minutes

Fresh Coriander Sauce with Pasta Bows

2 tablespoons olive oil	125 g/4 oz shallots, chopped finely
300 g/10 oz dried pasta bows	250 g/8 oz half-fat cream cheese
1 large bunch of coriander	125 ml/4 fl oz milk or single cream
50 g/2 oz pine nuts	salt and pepper

1 Bring at least 1.75 litres/3 pints water to the boil in a large saucepan. Add a dash of oil and a generous pinch of salt. Cook the pasta for 8-12 minutes, until just tender.

2 Meanwhile strip all the leaves from the coriander stalks. Set some of the leaves aside for the garnish. Chop the rest finely and place them in a mortar with the pine nuts. Crush with a pestle. Alternatively, combine the leaves and nuts in a bowl, and use the end of a rolling pin to crush the mixture.

3 Heat the remaining oil in a saucepan. Add the shallots and fry for 2 minutes, stirring constantly. Lower the heat and stir in the coriander mixture with the cream cheese and then the milk or cream. Add salt and pepper to taste and simmer for 2 minutes or until thoroughly heated through.

4 Drain the pasta and return it to the clean saucepan. Add the sauce and stir well to coat the pasta. Serve at once, garnished with the reserved coriander leaves.

Serves 4

Preparation time: 10 minutes
Cooking time: 12 minutes

VARIATIONS

Coriander Pasta Soufflés

1 Halve the ingredients in the main recipe, omitting the milk or cream and adding 4 eggs. Cook the pasta and make the coriander sauce as in the main recipe, adding 4 egg yolks and 50 g/2 oz grated Gruyère cheese instead of the milk or cream in step 3.

2 Remove the pan from the heat immediately and beat well.

3 Drain the pasta bows, tip them into a bowl, and then stir in the sauce. In a grease-free bowl, whisk the egg whites until soft peaks form. Using a large metal spoon, fold them into the pasta mixture, using a 'figure-of-eight' movement.

4 Grease 6 x 150 ml/¼ pint individual soufflé dishes and divide the soufflé mixture between them. Place on a baking sheet and cook in a preheated oven, 200°C (400°F), Gas Mark 6 for 15 minutes or until the soufflés are well risen and golden. Serve at once.

Serves 4

Preparation time: 20 minutes
Cooking time: 15 minutes
Oven temperature: 200°C (400°F),
Gas Mark 6

Lentil and Tomato Sauce with Tagliatelle

Keep checking the lentils as they cook, because the cooking time will vary according to their age and condition of storage. For a particularly sumptuous version of this dish, use Lentilles du Puy, *the caviar of lentils!*

250 g/8 oz green lentils, or
  Lentilles du Puy
1 tablespoon olive oil
1 onion, chopped
2 garlic cloves, crushed
1 x 397 g/14 oz can Italian
  plum tomatoes
2 tablespoons tomato purée
600 ml/1 pint hot vegetable stock
250 g/8 oz fresh tagliatelle
salt and pepper
1 tablespoon chopped fresh basil,
  to garnish

1 Bring a large saucepan of water to the boil. Add the lentils and boil rapidly for 10 minutes. Drain them, and set aside.

2 Heat the oil in a large frying pan. Add the onion and garlic and fry for 3-5 minutes until softened but not coloured, stirring constantly.

3 Add the lentils. Stir-fry for 1 minute, then stir in the tomatoes with the can juices, the tomato purée and stock. Add salt and pepper to taste. Simmer, uncovered, for 45 minutes until reduced by half, stirring occasionally to break up the tomatoes.

4 Meanwhile, bring at least 1.75 litres/3 pints water to the boil in a large saucepan. Add a dash of oil and a generous pinch of salt. Cook the pasta for 4-6 minutes, or until it rises to the surface of the boiling water.

5 Drain the pasta and tip it on to a large, heated platter. Season with black pepper and spoon the lentil and tomato sauce over. Garnish with the chopped basil.

Serves 4
Preparation time: 10 minutes
Cooking time: 1-1¼ hours

Pasta with Citrus Crème Fraîche

olive oil, see method
300 g/10 oz fresh tagliatelle verdi
1 x 250 g/8 oz tub crème fraîche
1 tablespoon grated lemon rind
1 tablespoon lemon juice
2 tablespoons chopped fresh
   parsley
salt and pepper

TO GARNISH:
strips of lemon rind
parsley sprigs

1 Boil at least 1.75 litres/3 pints water in a large saucepan with a dash of oil and a pinch of salt. Cook the pasta for 4-6 minutes, until it rises to the surface of the boiling water.
2 Meanwhile place the crème fraîche in a saucepan with the lemon rind and juice. Stir over very low heat until the crème fraîche becomes creamy. Stir in the parsley, with salt and pepper to taste.
3 Drain the pasta. Return to the clean pan and drizzle with olive oil. Pour in the sauce. Toss well and serve at once, garnished with the strips of lemon rind and parsley.

Serves 4
Preparation time: 5 minutes
Cooking time: 6 minutes

Crispy Bacon Pappardelle

1 tablespoon olive oil
1 onion, sliced
125 g/4 oz chorizo (spicy Spanish) sausage, sliced
375 g/12 oz dried pappardelle or other broad egg noodles
2 large ripe tomatoes
1 tablespoon chopped fresh coriander
8 rindless unsmoked back bacon rashers, grilled and cut into strips
salt
sprigs of coriander, to garnish

1 Heat the oil in a very large saucepan and add the onion. Fry for 5 minutes until softened but not coloured. Add the chorizo sausage and fry for 5 minutes more, stirring occasionally.
2 Meanwhile, bring at least 1.75 litres/3 pints water to the boil in a large saucepan. Add a dash of oil and a generous pinch of salt. Cook the pasta for 8-12 minutes, until just tender.
3 While the pasta is cooking, prepare the tomatoes. Bring a saucepan of water to the boil. Make a cross at the base of each tomato and plunge them into the water for 30 seconds. Remove with a slotted spoon and plunge them into cold water. Drain and peel off the skins. Cut the tomatoes in half and remove the seeds. Chop the flesh into large chunks. Add it to the sausage mixture with the coriander. Fry for a further 5 minutes. Add the bacon.
4 Drain the pasta, drizzle with a little oil and add to the sausage mixture. Stir and serve, garnished with sprigs of coriander.

Serves 4
Preparation time: 15 minutes
Cooking time: 25 minutes

Tagliatelle Bolognese

1 tablespoon olive oil
1 onion, chopped
2 garlic cloves, crushed
375 g/12 oz lean minced beef
2 tablespoons tomato purée
1 tablespoon chopped mixed
   fresh herbs
1 x 397 g/14 oz can chopped tomatoes
1 teaspoon Worcestershire sauce
150 ml/¼ pint hot beef stock
oil, see method
375 g/12 oz dried tagliatelle, plain, or
   made with spinach
salt and pepper
basil leaves, to garnish

1 Heat the oil in a large saucepan, add the onion and garlic and fry for 5 minutes until softened. Stir in the meat. Increase the heat and fry for 3 minutes, stirring constantly.

2 Reduce the heat, add the tomato purée and herbs and stir well. Add the tomatoes with the can juices, and stir in the Worcestershire sauce and stock. Simmer, covered, for 1 hour, stirring occasionally, until the sauce is rich and thickened. Add salt and pepper to taste.

3 About 10 minutes before the end of the cooking time, bring at least 1.75 litres/3 pints water to the boil in a large saucepan. Add a dash of oil and a generous pinch of salt. Cook the pasta for 8-12 minutes, until just tender. Drain, drizzle with a little more olive oil and season with black pepper.

4 Place the pasta on serving plates and spoon the sauce over. Garnish with basil and serve. Good country bread and a mixed green salad are suitable accompaniments.

Serves 4
Preparation time: 30 minutes
Cooking time: about 1¼ hours

Lamb and Pasta Bake

1 onion, sliced thinly into rings
250 g/8 oz cooked lean lamb, cubed
1 x 397 g/14 oz can chopped tomatoes
4 tablespoons tomato purée
2 tablespoons mixed dried herbs
1 x 397 g/14 oz can red kidney
   beans, drained
1 teaspoon cornflour
1 tablespoon water
175 g/6 oz dried macaroni, cooked
salt and pepper
TOPPING:
75 g/3 oz Cheddar cheese, grated
75 g/3 oz wholemeal breadcrumbs

1 Grease the base and sides of a
1.75 litre/3 pint ovenproof dish.
Dry fry the onion rings in a non-stick
frying pan for 3 minutes until
softened. Transfer to a bowl and mix
in the lamb, tomatoes, tomato purée,
herbs and kidney beans.
2 In a cup, mix the cornflour and
water to form a smooth paste. Stir
into the meat mixture, with the
cooked pasta. Season to taste.
3 Spoon the lamb mixture into the
prepared dish. Top with the mixed
cheese and breadcrumbs. Bake in a
preheated oven, 200°C (400°F),
Gas Mark 6, for 45 minutes, covering the dish with foil after 30 minutes
if the topping starts to overbrown.

Serves 4
Preparation time: 20 minutes
Cooking time: 45 minutes
Oven temperature: 200°C (400°F),
Gas Mark 6

Parmesan Meatballs

1 onion, grated
50 g/2 oz Parmesan cheese, grated
500 g/1 lb lean minced lamb
1 tablespoon tomato purée
1 teaspoon chilli sauce
1 tablespoon mixed dried herbs
4 tablespoons olive oil
375 g/12 oz dried spaghetti
salt and pepper

SAUCE:
1 tablespoon olive oil
1 onion, finely chopped
2 garlic cloves, crushed
1 x 397 g/14 oz can chopped
   tomatoes with herbs
2 tablespoons tomato purée
2 tablespoons chopped fresh oregano
oregano leaves, to garnish

1 Make the meatballs. In a bowl combine the onion, the Parmesan cheese, minced lamb, tomato purée, chilli sauce and herbs. Add salt and pepper, and mix thoroughly.
2 Using dampened hands divide and shape the mixture into 30 small balls. Heat the oil in a large frying pan and fry the meatballs in 2 batches for 10 minutes each. Using a slotted spoon, transfer the meatballs to a baking dish. Keep hot.
3 Bring at least 1.75 litres/3 pints water to the boil in a large saucepan. Add a dash of oil and a generous pinch of salt. Cook the pasta for 8-12 minutes, until just tender.
4 Meanwhile make the sauce. Heat the oil in a frying pan, add the onion and garlic and fry for 3-5 minutes until softened. Stir in the tomatoes, tomato purée and oregano. Simmer the sauce for 8 minutes.
5 Drain the pasta, pile it in a heated bowl and drizzle with a little more oil. Season with black pepper. Pour over the sauce and toss lightly. Serve with the meatballs, garnished with oregano.

Serves 4
Preparation time: 20 minutes
Cooking time: 32 minutes

Coriander and Chive Meatballs

Replace the dried herbs in the main recipe with 1 bunch finely chopped coriander and 1 bunch snipped chives. Add 125 g/4 oz very finely chopped mushrooms to the meatball mixture. Continue as for the main recipe.

Indian Meatballs with Tomato Curry Sauce

1 Cook the pasta and meatballs as in the main recipe, substituting 1 tablespoon each of ground cumin and coriander for the dried herbs.
2 To make the sauce, fry the onion and garlic as in the main recipe, then stir in 1 tablespoon Madras curry powder, 2 tablespoons tomato purée and 1 x 397 g/14 oz can chopped tomatoes. Omit the oregano in the original recipe.
3 Simmer the sauce, uncovered, for 5-10 minutes, then sprinkle in 2 teaspoons garam masala followed by 2 tablespoons chopped fresh coriander. Stir. Serve at once, with the pasta and meatballs.

Dry-fry Mince Rigatoni

Unlike a bolognaise sauce, in which the mince is fully integrated with the other ingredients, this method of cooking results in a very rustic-looking mixture with plenty of body and bite.

375 g/12 oz lean minced beef
1 tablespoon black pepper
1 teaspoon cocoa powder
1 teaspoon garlic salt
1 teaspoon piri piri seasoning
15 g/½ oz plain flour
oil, see method
375 g/12 oz dried rigatoni
2 tablespoons chopped fresh parsley
50 g/2 oz Parmesan cheese
salt and pepper

1 In a bowl, combine the minced beef, pepper, cocoa, garlic salt, piri piri seasoning and flour. Using your hands, mix so the mince becomes coated in the spiced flour, but is still free-flowing. The aim is not to produce a dense meat loaf mixture, but to keep the mince strands separate as much as possible.
2 Heat a non-stick frying pan and add the mince in uneven spoonfuls. Fry over high heat, turning the mounds over with a spatula, for 10 minutes until crisp.
3 Meanwhile, bring 1.75 litres/ 3 pints water to the boil in a large saucepan. Add a dash of oil and a generous pinch of salt. Cook the pasta for about 8-12 minutes, until just tender.
4 Drain the pasta and add a little more olive oil. Stir into the mince mixture. Serve with chopped parsley and shavings of Parmesan cheese.

Serves 4
Preparation time: 5 minutes
Cooking time: 20 minutes

Mangetout and Beef Stir-fry

Fresh root ginger is readily available at many large supermarkets. Select a firm creamy root with no blemishes, break off the amount you need and store the rest in a plastic bag in the refrigerator.

25 g/1 oz fresh root ginger, shredded
1 garlic clove, crushed
4 tablespoons soy sauce
2 tablespoons dry sherry
1 teaspoon chilli sauce
1 teaspoon clear honey
½ teaspoon Chinese
   five-spice powder
500 g /1 lb fillet steak, sliced finely
1 tablespoon sesame oil
250 g/8 oz dried egg noodles
250 g/8 oz mangetout, trimmed
salt and pepper
TO GARNISH:
spring onions
carrot flowers (optional)

1 Combine the ginger, garlic, soy sauce, sherry, chilli sauce, honey and five-spice powder in a non-metallic bowl. Stir well. Add the beef, stir to coat thoroughly; marinate until required.

2 Boil at least 1.75 litres/3 pints water in a large saucepan. Add a dash of oil and a pinch of salt. Add the noodles, remove pan from the heat, cover and stand for 5 minutes.

3 Meanwhile heat a wok or large frying pan. Add the oil. When the oil is hot transfer the meat to the wok using a slotted spoon. Stir fry for about 3 minutes.

4 Add the mangetout and the marinade to the wok or pan, with salt and pepper if required. Stir-fry for a further 2 minutes.

5 Drain the noodles and arrange them on a platter. Spoon the stir-fry over the top. Garnish with shredded spring onions or carrot flowers – made by scoring peeled carrots lengthways at regular intervals, then cutting them into slices.

Serves 4
Preparation time: 10 minutes
Cooking time: 5 minutes

Lasagne

This is the sort of lasagne which is best eaten with a spoon. Serve good crusty bread to mop up the juices.

9 dried 'no-precook' lasagne sheets
50 g/2 oz Parmesan cheese, grated

MEAT SAUCE:

2 tablespoons olive oil
2 onions, chopped finely
3 garlic cloves, crushed
1 tablespoon dried oregano
1 tablespoon dried basil
3 tablespoons tomato purée

500 g/1 lb lean minced beef
1 x 397 g/14 oz can plum tomatoes

CHEESE SAUCE:

600 ml/1 pint skimmed milk
1 onion, halved
4 cloves
25 g/1 oz butter
25 g/1 oz plain flour
250 g/8 oz Cheddar cheese, grated

1 Make the meat sauce. Heat the oil in a large saucepan and fry the onions for 3-5 minutes until softened. Add the garlic and fry for 1 minute more, then stir in the herbs, tomato purée and beef. Fry the mixture, stirring constantly for 5 minutes. Add the tomatoes to the filling with salt and pepper to taste. Stir well. Cover the pan and simmer the meat sauce for 45 minutes, stirring occasionally.

2 Meanwhile infuse the milk for the cheese sauce. Stick the cloves in the onion halves and put them in a small saucepan. Add the milk and bring to just below boiling point. Remove the pan from the heat and set aside for 15 minutes. Remove the onion halves and cloves.

3 Melt the butter in a saucepan. Stir in the flour and cook for 1 minute. Add the skimmed milk gradually, whisking or beating the sauce over moderate heat until thickened. Add the Cheddar cheese, stir well until melted, then stir in salt and pepper to taste. Set aside.

4 Grease the base and sides of an oval or rectangular 1.75 litre/3 pint ovenproof dish. Spoon one-third of the meat mixture over the base. Spread over a quarter of the cheese sauce and cover with 3 sheets of lasagne.

5 Repeat the layering process twice more, finishing with a layer of pasta. Cover with the remaining cheese sauce. Sprinkle over the Parmesan. Bake the lasagne in a preheated oven, 190°C (375°F), Gas Mark 5, for 1 hour. Serve with a green salad and crusty bread.

Serves 4
Preparation time: 1 hour
Cooking time: 1 hour

VARIATIONS

Lasagne Verdi

Replace the plain lasagne with the same quantity of lasagne verdi (spinach-flavoured lasagne). Replace the tomato purée with the same quantity of ready-made pesto or 3 tablespoons chopped fresh basil. Proceed as for the main recipe.

Chicken Lasagne

Replace the minced beef with the same quantity of lean minced chicken. Replace half the milk with natural yogurt when making the cheese sauce. Proceed as for the main recipe.

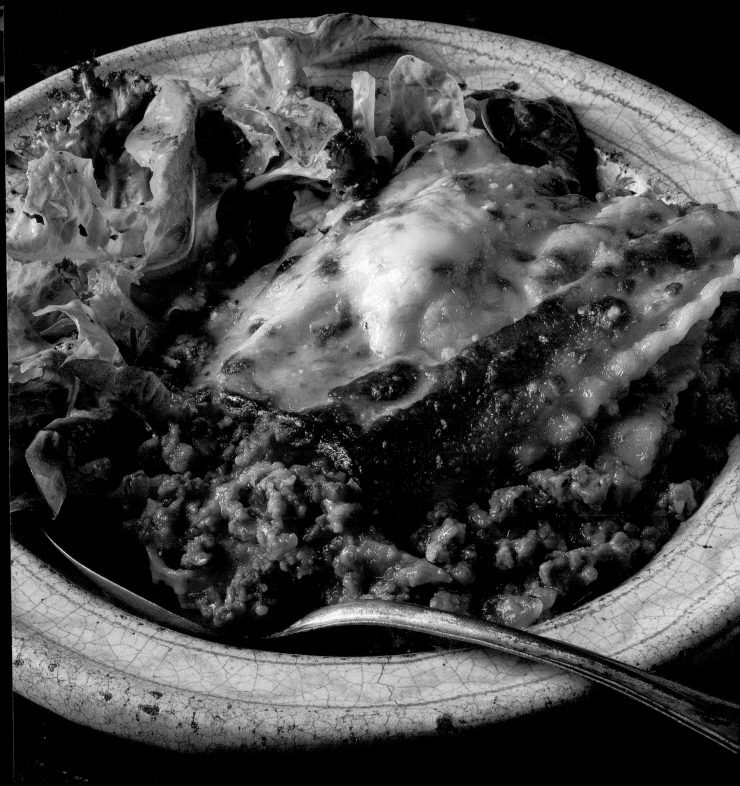

1 Heat the oil and butter in a saucepan. Add the onion and carrot and fry for 5 minutes. Stir in the plain flour and cook for about 1 minute, stirring constantly. Stir in the tomato purée and stock, with salt and pepper to taste. Simmer for 20 minutes.

2 Meanwhile bring 1.75 litres/ 3 pints water to the boil in a large saucepan. Add a dash of oil and a generous pinch of salt. Cook the pasta for about 8-12 minutes, until just tender.

3 Press the tomato sauce through a fine metal sieve into a clean saucepan. Add the ham and mushrooms and heat through.

4 Drain the pasta, pile it into a heated dish and pour the sauce over. Serve with the grated Parmesan cheese.

Serves 4
Preparation time: 20 minutes
Cooking time: 26 minutes

Spaghetti Milanese

1 tablespoon olive oil
15 g/½ oz butter
1 onion, chopped
1 carrot, chopped
15 g/½ oz plain flour
4 tablespoons tomato purée

450 ml/¾ pint hot vegetable stock, or chicken stock
250 g/8 oz dried spaghetti
50 g/2 oz lean ham, sliced into thin strips
75 g/3 oz button mushrooms, thinly sliced
salt and pepper
25 g/1 oz Parmesan cheese, grated, to serve

Mexican Chilli Shell Bake

1 tablespoon olive oil
2 garlic cloves, crushed
1 onion, chopped finely
1 green chilli, deseeded and chopped
250 g/8 oz lean minced beef
2 teaspoons mild chilli powder
3 tablespoons tomato purée
250 g/8 oz dried wholemeal
   pasta shells
150 g/5 oz mozzarella cheese, grated
75 g/3 oz Cheddar cheese, grated
2 eggs, beaten
salt and pepper

1 Heat the oil in a heavy-based saucepan. Add the garlic and onion and fry for about 5 minutes, stirring occasionally until softened.
2 Add the chilli and minced beef. Fry for 5 minutes, stirring constantly. Stir in the chilli powder and the tomato purée, with salt and pepper to taste. Simmer, partially covered, for about 25 minutes to form a dry spicy sauce.
3 Meanwhile bring at least 1.75 litres/3 pints water to the boil in a large saucepan. Add a dash of oil and a generous pinch of salt. Cook the pasta for 8-12 minutes, until just tender. Drain the pasta and transfer it to a 1.75 litre/3 pint ovenproof dish. Pour the sauce over the pasta and mix well.
4 Mix the cheeses with the egg in a bowl; pour over the mixture. Bake in a preheated oven, 190°C (375°F), Gas Mark 5, for 20 minutes.

Serves 4
Preparation time: 45 minutes
Cooking time: 20 minutes
Oven temperature: 190°C (375°F), Gas Mark 5

Chicken and Orange Shells

250 g/8 oz cooked chicken breast,
  roughly chopped
grated rind of 1 orange
2 tablespoons orange juice
1 egg, separated
3 tablespoons double cream
½ teaspoon cayenne pepper

16 large dried pasta shells, cooked
1 bag mixed salad leaves (4 portions)
4 tablespoons olive oil
salt and pepper
TO GARNISH:
sprigs of fennel
basil leaves

1 Combine the chicken, orange rind, juice, egg yolk, cream and cayenne in a food processor. Add salt and pepper to taste. Process for 1 minute or until smooth. Whisk the egg white in a grease-free bowl until firm peaks form; fold into the chicken mixture.
2 Spoon a little of the filling into each pasta shell. Arrange the shells over the base of a steamer and steam for 15 minutes or until the chicken filling has set.
3 Arrange the salad leaves on 4 serving plates and place the shells on top. Drizzle with the olive oil and garnish with the fennel sprigs and basil leaves.

Serves 4
Preparation time: 10 minutes
Cooking time: 15 minutes

VARIATIONS

Pine Nut and Orange Shells

Follow steps 1 and 2 of the main recipe, adding 25 g/1 oz pine nuts when processing the chicken. Heat 1 tablespoon of oil in a saucepan. Fry 1 chopped onion and 1 crushed garlic clove for 3 minutes until softened. Add 1 x 397 g/14 oz chopped tomatoes, with salt and pepper to taste. Simmer for 15 minutes. Omit the lettuce leaves and serve the pasta with the sauce.

Tomato and Orange Shells with Cheese Sauce

Follow steps 1 and 2 of the main recipe, but substitute tomato pasta shells. For the cheese sauce, melt 25 g/1 oz butter in a saucepan. Stir in 25 g/1 oz plain flour and cook for 1 minute. Gradually add 300 ml/½ pint milk, whisking or beating the sauce until thickened. Stir in 175 g/6 oz grated Cheddar cheese until melted. Place the steamed pasta shells in a flameproof dish. Pour the sauce over the top and place under a hot grill for 5 minutes until the topping is golden brown. Serve at once.

Spicy Chicken Pipe Rigate

'Pipe' are curved elbow-shaped pasta shapes, and these have the ribbed or 'rigate' surface, which is designed to take up large quantities of sauce. Pipe rigate are best suited to sauces which contain chicken, meat, cheese and/or cream, or tomato.

1 teaspoon chilli powder
1 teaspoon cayenne pepper
1 teaspoon turmeric
1 tablespoon olive oil
250 g/8 oz skinned chicken breast,
    cut into bite-sized pieces
1 onion, chopped
1 x 397 g/14 oz can plum tomatoes
1 teaspoon caster sugar
1 bunch of fresh basil
375 g/12 oz dried pipe rigate
salt and pepper

1 In a bowl, mix together the chilli powder, cayenne, turmeric and 1 teaspoon of the olive oil. Stir to form a paste. Add the chicken pieces and coat thoroughly in the spice mixture. Cover and set aside for 15 minutes.
2 Meanwhile, heat the remaining olive oil in a large frying pan. Add the onion and fry for 3 minutes until softened but not coloured. Add the tomatoes and sugar. Strip the basil leaves from the stems. Set some leaves aside for the garnish. Chop the rest finely and add them to the pan. Boil the mixture rapidly for 5 minutes. Stir occasionally to break up the tomatoes.
3 Bring 1.75 litres/3 pints water to the boil in a large saucepan. Add a dash of oil and a generous pinch of salt. Cook the pasta for about 8-12 minutes, until just tender.
4 Meanwhile, dry-fry the spicy chicken pieces in a non-stick frying pan for 10 minutes or until crisp. Add to the sauce. Drain the pasta, drizzle with a little more oil and add salt and pepper. Arrange the pasta on a large serving platter and pour over the sauce. Serve garnished with the reserved basil leaves.

Serves 4
Preparation time: 15 minutes, plus 15 minutes marinating time
Cooking time: 25-30 minutes

Spinach and Chicken Cannelloni

12 dried cannelloni tubes
60 g/2 oz Cheddar cheese, grated

FILLING:

250 g/8 oz fresh leaf spinach
1 tablespoon olive oil
1 onion, chopped finely
250 g/8 oz cooked chicken
    breast, minced
125 g/4 oz ricotta cheese
1 teaspoon ground cinnamon
salt and pepper

TOMATO SAUCE:

1 tablespoon olive oil
1 onion, chopped finely
1 tablespoon chopped fresh oregano
300 ml/½ pint passata
    (sieved tomatoes)
½ teaspoon caster sugar

CHEESE SAUCE:

15 g/½ oz butter
15 g/½ oz plain flour
300 ml/½ pint skimmed milk
175 g/6 oz Cheddar cheese, grated

1 Prepare the filling. Wash the spinach thoroughly and remove any tough stalks. Put it into a large saucepan with just the water that clings to the leaves. Cook over low heat for 5 minutes or until the leaves have wilted and the water has evaporated. Strain the spinach and squeeze out all the excess liquid, pressing the spinach against the side of the strainer with a wooden spoon. Chop the spinach finely and transfer it to a bowl.

2 Heat the oil in a pan and fry the onion for 3-5 minutes until softened. Add to the spinach with the chicken, ricotta and cinnamon, and season to taste. Stir the filling well and spoon it into the cannelloni tubes. Arrange the filled tubes in a single layer on the base of a rectangular 1.2 litre/2 pint ovenproof dish.

3 Make the tomato sauce. Heat the oil in a frying pan and fry the onion for 3-5 minutes until softened. Stir in the oregano, passata and sugar and simmer for 15 minutes.

4 Make the cheese sauce. Melt the butter in a saucepan, stir in the flour and cook for 1 minute. Add the milk gradually, whisking or beating the sauce over moderate heat until thickened. Add the cheese and stir until melted.

5 Pour the tomato sauce over the filled cannelloni, followed by the cheese sauce. Sprinkle the grated cheese over the top. Bake in a preheated oven, 190°C (375°F), Gas Mark 5, for 45 minutes. Serve at once.

Serves 4
Preparation time: 20 minutes
Cooking time: 1¼ hours
Oven temperature: 190°C (375°F),
Gas Mark 5

Pork Schnitzels with Pappardelle

4 pork escalopes, about
   125 g/4 oz each
1 egg
125 g/4 oz fresh white breadcrumbs
75 g/3 oz butter
2 tablespoons vegetable oil

250 g/8 oz dried pappardelle or other
   broad egg noodles
50 g/2 oz anchovy fillets, chopped
150 ml/¼ pint double cream
2 tablespoons chopped fresh oregano
salt and pepper

1 Place the pork between 2 sheets of greaseproof paper and flatten with a meat mallet or rolling pin until double their original size.
2 Beat the egg together with the salt and pepper in a shallow bowl. Spread out the breadcrumbs on a sheet of foil. Dip each schnitzel in the egg then coat in the breadcrumbs. Melt the butter with the oil in a large frying pan. Fry the schnitzels for 15 minutes, turning once.
3 Meanwhile, bring at least 1.75 litres/3 pints water to the boil in a large saucepan. Add a dash of oil and a generous pinch of salt. Cook the pasta for about 8-12 minutes, until just tender.
4 Remove the pork from the pan and drain on paper towels. Keep hot.
5 Drain the pasta, and return it to the clean saucepan. Add the anchovies, cream and oregano. Toss well. Arrange the pasta on a large heated platter and serve with the schnitzels.

Serves 4
Preparation time: 20 minutes
Cooking time: 15 minutes

VARIATIONS

Pork Schnitzels with Paprika Sauce

Cook the schnitzels and pasta as for the main recipe. Meanwhile, heat 1 tablespoon olive oil in a large frying pan. Add 1 red and 1 yellow pepper, (cored, deseeded, and sliced into rings). Fry for 3 minutes. Stir in 1 teaspoon paprika and 150 ml/¼ pint passata (sieved tomatoes). Simmer the sauce for 10 minutes and toss with the pasta instead of adding the anchovies, cream and herbs. Serve at once with the schnitzels.

Pork Schnitzels with Mushrooms

This is a variation on Pork Schnitzels with Paprika Sauce (above). Cook the schnitzels and pasta as before. Make the sauce, adding 15 g/½ oz butter when heating the oil in the frying pan. Add 125 g/4 oz sliced button mushrooms and 50 g/2 oz sliced shiitake mushrooms to the pepper mixture. Omit the paprika when adding the passata. Simmer the sauce for 10 minutes before tossing it with the pasta. Serve with the schnitzels.

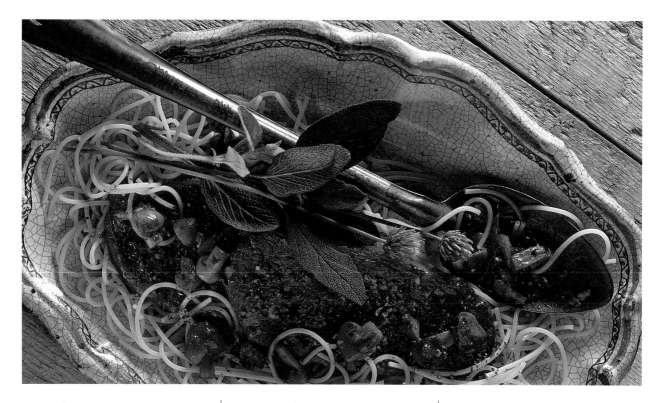

Garlic Spaghetti with Beef

375 g/12 oz dried garlic spaghetti
2½ tablespoons olive oil
2 tablespoons mixed
whole peppercorns
4 sirloin steaks, about 250 g/8 oz each
25 g/1 oz butter
1 teaspoon Dijon mustard
125 ml/4 fl oz red wine
125 g/4 oz button mushrooms,
finely chopped
salt and pepper
mixed fresh herbs, to garnish

1 Bring at least 1.75 litres/3 pints water to the boil in a large saucepan. Add a dash of oil and a generous pinch of salt. Cook the pasta for about 8-12 minutes, until just tender.

2 Meanwhile, crush the peppercorns and pat them over each steak. Melt the butter in the oil in a large frying pan and fry the steaks for 7 minutes, turning once.

3 Add the mustard, red wine and the chopped mushrooms to the pan, with salt and pepper to taste. Simmer for 5 minutes until the sauce has reduced slightly.

4 Drain the pasta and arrange it on a large, heated platter. Top with the steaks and pour over the sauce. Garnish with mixed fresh herbs and serve at once.

Serves 4
Preparation time: 15 minutes
Cooking time: 12 minutes

Chunky Gammon Farfalle

'Farfalle' is the Italian name for butterflies, and it is said that they foretell the coming of spring. But pasta butterflies are good at any time of year, and this cheese and gammon sauce makes a good winter dish too.

2 tablespoons olive oil
1 onion, chopped
1 red pepper, cored, deseeded and diced finely
250 g/8 oz cooked gammon, diced
500 g/1 lb dried farfalle
50 g/2 oz Cheddar cheese, finely grated
150 ml/¼ pint double cream
2 tablespoons chopped fresh parsley
salt and pepper
flat leaf parsley sprigs, to garnish

1 Heat 1 tablespoon of the oil in a large frying pan. Add the onion and fry for 5 minutes until softened but not coloured. Add the red pepper and gammon pieces; fry for 10 minutes or until crisp.

2 Meanwhile, bring at least 1.75 litres/3 pints water to the boil in a large saucepan. Add a dash of oil and a generous pinch of salt. Cook the pasta for 8-12 minutes until just tender.

3 Add the Cheddar cheese, cream and parsley to the gammon mixture. Simmer, stirring occasionally, for about 5 minutes. Add salt and pepper to taste. Drain the cooked pasta and add it to the pan. Toss lightly and serve, garnished with flat leaf parsley.

Serves 4
Preparation time: 15 minutes
Cooking time: 15-20 minutes

Green Chilli Chicken with Spinach Tagliarini

4 boneless, skinless chicken breasts, each about 125 g/4 oz
1 tablespoon olive oil
2 green chillies, deseeded and sliced
1 green pepper, cored, deseeded and sliced
1 teaspoon lime juice
1 x 397 g/14 oz can chopped Italian tomatoes
50 g/2 oz stoned black olives
50 g/2 oz stoned green olives
250 g/8 oz dried spinach tagliarini
salt and pepper
flat leaf parsley, to garnish

1 Cut each chicken breast into 4 pieces. Heat a wok or large frying pan. Add the oil. When hot, add the chicken pieces, chillies and green pepper. Stir-fry for about 5 minutes or until the chicken has browned.

2 Stir in the lime juice, tomatoes and olives, with salt and pepper to taste. Reduce the heat and simmer the sauce for 15 minutes.

3 Meanwhile bring at least 1.75 litres/3 pints water to the boil in a large saucepan. Add a dash of oil and a generous pinch of salt. Cook the pasta for about 8-12 minutes, until just tender.

4 Drain the pasta. Pile it on a large heated platter and spoon over the chicken mixture. Garnish with flat leaf parsley and serve at once.

Serves 4
Preparation time: 10 minutes
Cooking time: 20 minutes

Spaghetti Marinara

The wine and stock in the velouté sauce gives this dish a dinner party feel. You can use milk instead of wine if you prefer.

oil, see method
300 g/10 oz dried spaghetti
25 g/1 oz butter
25 g/1 oz plain flour
125 ml/4 fl oz dry white wine
125 ml/4 fl oz hot vegetable stock
125 g/4 oz fresh squid, cut into rings
125 g/4 oz salmon steak, boned and cubed
50 g/2 oz fresh or frozen peeled prawns, thawed
salt and pepper
1 tablespoon chopped fresh fennel fronds, to garnish

1 Bring at least 1.75 litres/3 pints water to the boil in a large saucepan. Add a dash of oil and a generous pinch of salt. Cook the pasta for 8-12 minutes.
2 Meanwhile, melt the butter in a saucepan, stir in the flour and cook for about 1 minute. Gradually add the wine and the stock, whisking or beating the sauce over moderate heat until thickened. Add salt and pepper to taste, stir in the squid, salmon and prawns, then simmer for 5 minutes.
3 Drain the pasta and return it to the clean saucepan. Add the fish sauce and toss lightly. Serve at once, garnished with the fennel fronds.

Serves 4
Preparation time: 20 minutes
Cooking time: 12 minutes

Tagliatelle with Garlic Mussels

1 tablespoon olive oil
300 g/10 oz dried tagliatelle
4 garlic cloves, crushed
1 kg/2 lb fresh mussels, scrubbed
   and bearded
pinch of saffron strands
250 ml/8 fl oz double cream
2 tablespoons chopped fresh dill
salt and pepper
dill sprigs, to garnish

1 Bring at least 1.75 litres/3 pints water to the boil in a large saucepan. Add a dash of oil and a pinch of salt. Cook the pasta for about 8-12 minutes, until just tender.
2 Heat the remaining oil in a large saucepan. Add the garlic and fry over gentle heat for 3 minutes, stirring constantly until softened.
3 Check over the mussels. Discard any which are open and do not close immediately when tapped.
4 Pound the saffron threads to a powder, and stir in 2-3 tablespoons of boiling water until dissolved. Stir into the garlic in the saucepan, add the mussels, cover and simmer for 5 minutes or until all the shells have opened. Discard any mussels with shells which remain shut.
5 Using a slotted spoon, remove the mussels from the pan. Set aside 10 whole mussels for garnish. Remove the remaining mussels from their shells and return them to the pan. Add the double cream and dill, with salt and pepper to taste. Simmer for 3 minutes.
6 Drain the pasta and add it to the mussel sauce. Toss well and serve garnished with the reserved whole mussels and dill sprigs.

Serves 4
Preparation time: 30 minutes
Cooking time: 15 minutes

Tuna Penne Bake

1 tablespoon olive oil
300 g/10 oz dried penne
1 onion, chopped
150 ml/¼ pint passata
   (sieved tomatoes)
2 tablespoons mixed dried herbs
1 x 200 g/7 oz can tuna in
   brine, drained
175 g/6 oz Cheddar cheese, grated
50 g/2 oz stoned black olives, halved
salt

1 Bring at least 1.75 litres/3 pints water to the boil in a large saucepan. Add a dash of oil and a pinch of salt. Cook the pasta for about 8-12 minutes, until just tender.
2 Meanwhile, heat the remaining oil in a saucepan. Fry the onion for about 3-5 minutes, stirring constantly until softened. Stir in the passata and mixed herbs.
3 Drain the pasta and place it in a lightly greased 1.2 litre/2 pint ovenproof dish. Scatter the tuna over the pasta. Pour the sauce over the tuna and sprinkle over the cheese. Scatter the olives on top. Bake in a preheated oven, 180°C (350°F), Gas Mark 4, for 30 minutes. Serve with a mixed leaf salad, if liked.

Serves 4
Preparation time: 20 minutes
Cooking time: 30 minutes
Oven temperature: 180°C (350°F),
Gas Mark 4

Spaghetti with Anchovies and Olives

oil, see method
375 g/12 oz dried spaghetti
25 g/1 oz butter
6 drained canned anchovy
   fillets, chopped
1 tablespoon tomato purée

1 tablespoon olive paste
6 stoned black olives, chopped
pepper
bunch of fresh basil
Parmesan shavings, to garnish

1 Bring at least 1.75 litres/3 pints water to the boil in a large saucepan. Add a dash of oil and a generous pinch of salt. Cook the pasta for 8-12 minutes, until just tender.
2 Drain the pasta and set it aside. Melt the butter in a large saucepan. Add the anchovy fillets, tomato purée, olive paste and olives. Stir over the heat until the mixture sizzles. Season well with pepper. Cool for 1 minute.
3 Add the drained pasta to the saucepan. Toss well. Tear the basil leaves and add them to the pasta. Serve with shavings of Parmesan.

Serves 4
Preparation time: 10 minutes
Cooking time: 12-14 minutes

VARIATIONS

Spaghetti with Tomato and Mussels

Make as for the main recipe, but substitute 250 g/8 oz chopped fresh plum tomatoes and about 50 g/2 oz drained canned mussels instead of the anchovies. Add 1 tablespoon each of chopped fresh parsley and oregano instead of the torn basil leaves when tossing the pasta with the sauce.

Spaghetti with Anchovies, Pesto and Balsamic Vinegar

Make as for the main recipe, omitting the olive paste and olives and adding 2 tablespoons of ready-made pesto and 1 tablespoon balsamic vinegar to the anchovies and tomato purée. Stir in 1 red pepper (cored, deseeded and chopped). Continue as for the main recipe, and serve with torn basil leaves and shavings of Parmesan.

Char-grilled Cod Steaks with Fettuccine

4 cod steaks, about 150 g/5 oz each
4 tablespoons olive oil
1 teaspoon lime juice
1 teaspoon soy sauce
300 g/10 oz dried fettuccine
2 tablespoons chopped fresh
   flat leaf parsley
salt and pepper
TO GARNISH:
lemon wedges
lime wedges
flat leaf parsley sprigs

1 Prepare a barbecue; alternatively, heat a griddle pan or non-stick frying pan. Brush each cod steak with a little oil. Drizzle over a little lime juice and soy sauce.
2 Cook the fish on a grill over hot coals, on the griddle, or in the frying pan for about 8 minutes on each side, or until cooked through.
3 Meanwhile, bring at least 1.75 litres/3 pints water to the boil in a large saucepan. Add a dash of oil and a generous pinch of salt. Cook the pasta for 8-12 minutes, until just tender.
4 Drain the fettuccine and return it to the clean pan. Add the chopped fresh parsley, and stir, then drizzle over a little more olive oil if liked. Toss well. Spoon the fettuccine on to heated plates and serve with the char-grilled fish. Garnish with wedges of lemon and lime, and sprigs of flat leaf parsley.

Serves 4
Preparation time: 10 minutes
Cooking time: 16 minutes

Lasagne Marinara

Lasagne is the wide strip pasta used in baked dishes, and is widely used in Neopolitan cooking. It is available plain or in green, which has been flavoured with spinach – and also with straight of frilled edges. This recipe is for a seafood lasagne and uses the 'no-pre-cook' variety, which has made life very much easier for the pasta cook.

9 dried, 'no-pre-cook' lasagne sheets
2 eggs, beaten
200 g/7 oz Cheddar cheese, grated
sprigs of dill, to garnish
SAUCE:
50 g/2 oz butter
50 g/2 oz plain flour
600 ml/1 pint milk
few saffron strands
salt and pepper
250 g/8 oz fresh salmon tail
125 g/4 oz cod fillet
125 g/4 oz fresh squid rings

1 Make the sauce. Melt the butter in a saucepan, stir in the flour and cook for 1 minute. Gradually add the milk, whisking or beating the sauce over moderate heat until it thickens. Pound the saffron threads to a powder in a bowl and stir in 2-3 tablespoons boiling water until dissolved. Add to the sauce, with salt and pepper to taste. Mix well.
2 Remove any bones from the salmon and cod and cut the fish into bite-sized pieces. Fold into the sauce with the squid rings. Remove from the heat.
3 Spoon one-third of the fish mixture over the base of a 1.75 litre/3 pint ovenproof dish, and then cover with a layer of lasagne sheets. Repeat these layers twice, finishing with a layer of pasta.
4 Beat the eggs and Cheddar cheese in a bowl. Add salt and pepper to taste and pour over the top of the lasagne.
5 Bake in a preheated oven at 190°C (375°F), Gas Mark 5, for 45 minutes, covering the dish with foil after 30 minutes if the surface starts to overbrown. Serve, garnished with sprigs of dill.

Serves 4
Preparation time: 20 minutes
Cooking time: 45 minutes
Oven temperature: 190°C (375°F), Gas Mark 5

Tagliatelle with Salmon Cream

oil, see method
425 g/14 oz dried tagliatelle
25 g/1 oz butter
1 garlic clove, crushed
1 onion, chopped
250 g/8 oz assorted mushrooms,
   sliced if large

250 g/8 oz salmon fillet, cubed
2 tablespoons snipped fresh chives
1 tablespoon chopped, fresh,
   flat leaf parsley
150 ml/¼ pint double cream
salt
flat leaf parsley sprigs, to garnish

1 Bring at least 1.75 litres/3 pints water to the boil in a large saucepan. Add a dash of oil and a generous pinch of salt. Cook the pasta for 8-12 minutes, until just tender.

2 Meanwhile, melt the butter in a frying pan. Add the garlic and onion and fry for about 3-5 minutes until softened but not browned.

3 Stir in the mushrooms. Fry for 4 minutes or until the mushrooms have softened. Reduce the heat and add the salmon pieces. Cook for 4 minutes or until the fish is beginning to flake. Stir in the herbs and cream.

4 Drain the pasta and return it to the clean saucepan. Add the sauce, stirring carefully until well mixed.

5 Garnish with flat leaf parsley and serve with a crunchy green salad and good French bread.

Serves 4
Preparation time: 20 minutes
Cooking time: 12-15 minutes

Seafood Pasta Twists

oil, see method
375 g/12 oz dried pasta twists
25 g/1 oz butter
125 g/4 oz peeled cooked prawns
125 g/4 oz fresh mussels, cooked
  and shelled
125 g/4 oz squid rings
300 ml/½ pint single cream
1 tablespoon chopped fresh dill
50 g/2 oz frozen sweetcorn
  niblets, thawed
25 g/1 oz oyster mushrooms, sliced
salt and pepper

TO GARNISH:
lemon wedges
flat leaf parsley sprigs

1 Bring at least 1.75 litres/3 pints water to the boil in a large saucepan. Add a dash of oil and a generous pinch of salt. Cook the pasta for about 8-12 minutes, until just tender.

2 Melt the butter in a saucepan. Add the cooked prawns and mussels and the squid rings. Fry for about 3 minutes, stirring from time to time. Stir in the cream, dill, sweetcorn and mushrooms, with salt and pepper to taste.

3 Drain the pasta and return to the clean pan. Add the sauce and stir carefully. Serve at once, garnished with the lemon wedges and parsley.

Serves 4
Preparation time: 10 minutes
Cooking time: 15 minutes

Gnocchi Fish Bake

500 g/1 lb Cyprus potatoes, peeled
½ teaspoon salt
1 egg, beaten
150 g/5 oz plain flour
lemon wedges, to garnish

FILLING:

a few saffron strands
300 ml/½ pint hot fish stock
50 g/2 oz butter
50 g/2 oz plain flour
250 g/8 oz peeled cooked prawns
125 g/4 oz salmon steak, skinned
   and cubed
125 g/4 oz cod steak, skinned
   and cubed
4 tablespoons double cream
2 tablespoons chopped fresh dill
salt and pepper

1 Cook potatoes in a saucepan of boiling water for 30 minutes or until tender enough to mash. Drain well and return to the pan. Mash the potatoes, then return the pan to a low heat to allow any excess liquid to evaporate. Beat in the egg and flour until smooth, then turn the mixture out on to a floured board. Shape into walnut-sized balls.

2 Boil 1.75 litres/3 pints water in a large saucepan. Add a dash of oil and salt. Cook the gnocchi, in 2 batches if necessary, for 3 minutes or until they all start to float to the surface. Drain well and keep hot.

3 Make the filling. In a small bowl, pound the saffron to a powder; and dissolve in a little fish stock. Melt the butter in a saucepan. Stir in the flour

and cook for 1 minute. Gradually whisk or beat in the saffron, with the remaining fish stock, over a moderate heat for 5 minutes until thickened. Season to taste.

4 Carefully stir the prawns, salmon and cod into the sauce, with the cream and dill, then spoon into a 1.2 litre/2 pint ovenproof dish.

5 Arrange the gnocchi over the fish, overlapping them slightly. Bake in a preheated oven, 180°C (350°F), Gas Mark 4, for 30 minutes. Serve garnished with lemon wedges.

Serves 4

Preparation time: 45 minutes
Cooking time: 1 hour 10 minutes
Oven temperature: 180°C (350°F), Gas Mark 4

Smoked Mussel and Angel Hair Bake

1 tablespoon olive oil
1 onion, chopped finely
1 x 397 g/14 oz can chopped
   tomatoes
150 ml/¼ pint passata (sieved
   tomatoes)
125 g/4 oz button mushrooms,
   chopped
2 tablespoons chopped fresh oregano

250 g/8 oz dried angel hair pasta
1 x 105 g/3½ oz can smoked
   mussels, drained
1 tablespoon capers, chopped
125 g/4 oz mature Cheddar
   cheese, grated
125 g/4 oz mozzarella cheese, sliced
2 large plum tomatoes, sliced
salt and pepper

1 Heat the oil in a frying pan, add the onion and fry for 3-5 minutes until softened. Add the canned tomatoes, passata, mushrooms and oregano with salt and pepper to taste. Simmer for 5 minutes.

2 Meanwhile, bring at least 1.75 litres/3 pints water to the boil in a large saucepan. Add a dash of oil and a generous pinch of salt. Cook the pasta for about 5-7 minutes, until just tender, then drain. Using scissors, snip the pasta into 2.5 cm/1 inch lengths.

3 Return the pasta to the clean pan. Add the tomato sauce with the smoked mussels and capers. Taste the mixture and add more salt and pepper if required.

4 Spoon half the mixture into a lightly greased 1.2 litre/2 pint ovenproof dish. Sprinkle over the Cheddar cheese and spoon the remaining mixture over the top. Cover with the mozzarella and tomato slices and bake in a preheated oven, 200°C (400°F), Gas Mark 6, for 30 minutes. Serve at once with crusty bread and a crisp green salad.

Serves 4
Preparation time: 20 minutes
Cooking time: 30 minutes
Oven temperature: 200°C (400°F), Gas Mark 6

Vegetable Bolognese

1 tablespoon olive oil
300 g/10 oz dried spaghetti
1 onion, chopped
1 x 200 g/7 oz can baby carrots, drained and diced
1 leek, trimmed, cleaned and sliced
2 celery sticks, sliced
1 x 397 g/14 oz can plum tomatoes, drained and roughly chopped
1 tablespoon tomato purée
1 teaspoon cayenne pepper
125 g/4 oz chestnut mushrooms, sliced
salt and pepper
basil leaves, to garnish

1 Bring at least 1.75 litres/3 pints water to the boil in a large saucepan. Add a dash of oil and a generous pinch of salt. Cook the pasta for about 8-12 minutes, until just tender.

2 Meanwhile, heat the remaining oil in a saucepan. Add the onion and fry over a low heat for 3-5 minutes, until softened. Add the carrots, leek and celery. Stir in the tomatoes, tomato purée, cayenne and mushrooms. Add salt and pepper to taste and simmer for 10 minutes.

3 Drain the spaghetti and return it to the clean pan. Add black pepper to taste. Using a large fork, roll bundles of the pasta into 4 nests. Place 1 nest on each heated serving plate. Spoon one-quarter of the sauce into each nest. Arrange the basil leaves around the nests and serve.

Serves 4
Preparation time: 15 minutes
Cooking time: 12 minutes

Pasta Bows with Garlic and Parsley

oil, see method
300 g/10 oz dried pasta bows
50 g/2 oz butter
2 large garlic cloves, crushed
1 yellow pepper, cored, deseeded
   and finely sliced
125 g/4 oz button mushrooms, sliced
4 tablespoons chopped fresh parsley
6 tablespoons crème fraîche
salt and pepper

1 Bring at least 1.75 litres/3 pints water to the boil in a large saucepan. Add a dash of oil and a generous pinch of salt. Cook the pasta for about 8-12 minutes, until just tender.
2 Meanwhile, melt the butter in a small frying pan. Add the garlic, yellow pepper and mushrooms. Fry for 3-5 minutes until softened, stirring occasionally. Add half the parsley and all the crème fraîche, with salt and pepper to taste. Stir well and simmer for 2 minutes to heat through.
3 Drain the pasta, return to the clean pan and drizzle with a little oil. Season with freshly ground black pepper. Pour over the sauce and toss well. Serve at once, garnished with the remaining parsley.

Serves 4
Preparation time: 12 minutes
Cooking time: 12 minutes

VARIATIONS
Cashew and Brie Pasta Bows

Cook the pasta as for the main recipe. Make the sauce, omitting the parsley. Stir in 50 g/2 oz Brie cheese (cubed) and 2 tablespoons each of chopped cashew nuts and chopped fresh basil. Proceed as in the main recipe.

Three-bean Pasta Bows

Cook the pasta as for the main recipe. Fry the garlic, pepper and mushrooms for 2 minutes, then add 1 chopped celery stick and 125 g/4 oz each drained canned borlotti, red kidney and black-eye beans. Cook for 3 minutes, stirring. Proceed as in the main recipe.

Aubergine Layer Bake

2 aubergines, sliced
25 g/1 oz salt
2 tablespoons olive oil
1 onion, chopped
1 tablespoon chopped fresh oregano
1 tablespoon chopped fresh basil
125 g/4 oz button mushrooms,
    cut into quarters
1 x 550 g/18 oz jar passata
    (sieved tomatoes)
8-9 fresh lasagne sheets
375 g/12 oz mozzarella cheese, sliced
125 g/4 oz Gruyère cheese, grated
salt and pepper

1 Spread out the aubergine slices on baking sheets. Sprinkle with the salt and set aside for 15 minutes.
2 Heat 1 tablespoon of the oil in a large frying pan. Add onion; fry for 3-5 minutes, stirring until softened. Add the herbs, mushrooms and passata. Simmer for 10 minutes, then add salt and pepper to taste.
3 Rinse the aubergine slices under plenty of cold water, drain and pat dry with paper towels.
4 Spread the aubergine on baking sheets. Brush with the remaining oil. Grill under high heat for 10 minutes, turning once. Remove from the heat.
5 Arrange 3 lasagne sheets on the base of a rectangular 1.2 litre/ 2 pint ovenproof dish, lightly greased. Spoon over one-third of the tomato sauce. Place a layer of aubergines on top, and add a third of the mozzarella and Gruyère.
6 Repeat the layers twice more. Cover with foil. Bake in a preheated oven, 190°C (375°F), Gas Mark 5, for 45 minutes. Remove foil after 20 minutes to brown the top.

Serves 4
Preparation time: 30 minutes
Cooking time: 50 minutes
Oven temperature: 190°C (375°F), Gas Mark 5

Vegetable Ragout with Vermicelli

1 tablespoon olive oil
2 garlic cloves, crushed
1 onion, chopped
1 carrot, chopped finely and blanched
1 celery stick, chopped
1 red pepper, cored, deseeded
  and chopped

4 ripe fresh plum tomatoes, chopped
3 tablespoons ready-made red pesto
375 g/12 oz dried vermicelli
salt and pepper
2 tablespoons chopped fresh parsley,
  to garnish

1 Heat the oil in a saucepan, add the garlic and onion and fry for 3-5 minutes until softened. Add the carrot and celery and fry for 5 minutes more. Stir in the red pepper, with plenty of salt and pepper. Fry for 10 minutes more, adding a little water if necessary.

2 Add the tomatoes and pesto to the red pepper mixture. Cook for 5 minutes, then taste and add more salt and pepper if required.

3 When the sauce is almost cooked, bring at least 1.75 litres/3 pints water to the boil in a large saucepan. Add a dash of oil and a generous pinch of salt. Cook the pasta for 3-4 minutes.

4 Drain the pasta, return it to the clean pan and season with a little black pepper. Pile it on to a heated platter. Spoon the sauce over, garnish with the chopped fresh parsley and serve.

Serves: 4
Preparation time: 10 minutes
Cooking time: 20 minutes

Three-cheese Macaroni

A truly rich dish – the perfect meal to come home to after a bracing walk in the country.

oil, see method
300 g/10 oz dried macaroni
25 g/1 oz butter
25 g/1 oz plain flour
250 ml/8 fl oz skimmed milk
125 g/4 oz Pecorino cheese, grated
125 g/4 oz Gouda cheese, grated
125 g/4 oz Emmental cheese, grated
salt and pepper
½ teaspoon cayenne pepper

1 Bring at least 1.75 litres/3 pints water to the boil in a large saucepan. Add a dash of oil and a pinch of salt. Cook the pasta for 8-12 minutes, until just tender.
2 Meanwhile, melt the butter in a saucepan. Stir in the flour and cook for 1 minute. Gradually add the milk, whisking or beating the sauce over moderate heat until thickened.
3 Add 50 g/2 oz of each of the cheeses and stir until melted. Stir in the salt, pepper and cayenne.
4 Drain the pasta and transfer it to a lightly greased 1.2 litre/2 pint ovenproof dish. Spoon the sauce over the top and sprinkle with the remaining cheese.
5 Bake in a preheated oven, at 190°C (375°F), Gas Mark 5, for 45 minutes.

Serves 4
Preparation time: 25 minutes
Cooking time: 45 minutes
Oven temperature: 190°C (375°F), Gas Mark 5

VARIATION

Macaroni with Crunchy Topping

Cook as in the main recipe, but before baking, mix 50 g/2 oz wholemeal breadcrumbs and 25 g/1 oz grated Parmesan in a bowl. Sprinkle the mixture over the top, cover with foil and bake as before for 30 minutes, removing the foil for the final 10 minutes to brown the topping.

Baked Stuffed Mushrooms

4 large field mushrooms
1 small onion, very finely chopped
50 g/2 oz mini macaroni, cooked
25 g/1 oz walnuts, chopped
1 tablespoon chopped fresh parsley
25 g/1 oz Cheddar cheese, cubed
1 tablespoon tomato purée
1 egg, beaten
1 tablespoon olive oil
salt and pepper
lemon wedges, to garnish

1 Chop the mushroom stalks finely. Peel the mushrooms if blemished, and grill for 5 minutes until just softened. Remove and set aside.
2 Put the chopped onion into a large bowl. Add the chopped mushroom stalk, cooked macaroni, walnuts, parsley, cheese and tomato purée. Mix well, and then add enough of the beaten egg to bind the mixture. Add salt and pepper to taste.
3 Divide the filling between the mushrooms, mounding the mixture up with a spoon. Drizzle over a little oil. Arrange the filled mushrooms, well apart on a grill pan.
4 Grill for 15-20 minutes until the top of the stuffing is crisp and has started to char at the edges, then serve, garnished with lemon wedges.

Serves 4
Preparation time: 10 minutes
Cooking time: 20 minutes

Spinach and Ricotta Lasagne Pie

PASTRY:

125 g/4 oz plain wholemeal flour
125 g/4 oz plain flour
pinch of salt
50 g/2 oz butter, cubed
50 g/2 oz white vegetable fat, cubed
25 g/1 oz Pecorino cheese, grated finely
1 egg, beaten

FILLING:

400 g/13 oz fresh leaf spinach
1 teaspoon garlic purée
250 g/8 oz ricotta cheese
1 teaspoon cayenne pepper
50 g/2 oz hazelnuts, chopped
4 eggs
6 fresh lasagne sheets
salt and pepper

1 Sift the flours and salt into a bowl. Add the butter and fat. Rub in with your fingertips until the mixture resembles fine breadcrumbs. Make a well in the centre and add the cheese and egg. Mix to a soft yet not sticky dough, adding a little chilled water if necessary. Wrap in a plastic bag and chill for 15 minutes.

2 Wash the spinach thoroughly and remove any tough stalks. Tear the leaves into small pieces and place in a large saucepan with just the water that clings to the leaves. Cook over moderate heat for 10 minutes or until all the water has evaporated. Strain the spinach and squeeze out all the excess liquid, pressing the spinach against the side of the strainer with a wooden spoon. Transfer to a a bowl. Stir in the garlic purée, ricotta, cayenne and hazelnuts. Beat 3 of the eggs in a bowl. Stir them into the mixture. Add salt and pepper to taste and mix well.

3 Bring at least 1.75 litres/3 pints water to the boil in a large saucepan. Add a dash of oil and a generous pinch of salt. Add the lasagne sheets, one at a time, and cook them for 5 minutes. Drain on paper towels.

4 Line the base of a deep 25 cm/10 inch pie plate with 3 of the partially cooked lasagne sheets. Spread half the filling over the pasta, and top with the remaining lasagne. Cover with the rest of the filling.

5 Roll out the pastry on a lightly floured surface to cover the top of the pie. Pinch the edges to seal. Beat the remaining egg in a small bowl; brush over the pastry.

6 Bake the pie in a preheated oven, 200°C (400°F), Gas Mark 6, for 15 minutes. Reduce the temperature to 180°C (350°F), Gas Mark 4 and bake for 20 minutes more. Serve with grilled Mediterranean vegetables and a quick tomato sauce, or with a crisp green salad dressed with lemon juice.

Serves 4-6
Preparation time: 20 minutes
Cooking time: 35 minutes
Oven temperature: 200°C (400°F), Gas Mark 6, then 180°C (350°F), Gas Mark 4

Asparagus and Mushroom Tagliatelle

225 g/8 oz fresh asparagus spears, cut into 2.5 cm/1 inch lengths, blanched
125 g/4 oz chestnut mushrooms, sliced
2.5 cm/1 inch piece of fresh root ginger, grated
25 g/1 oz butter
1 tablespoon chopped fresh tarragon
250 ml/8 fl oz double cream or crème fraîche.
oil, see method
300 g/10 oz fresh tagliatelle
salt and pepper

TO GARNISH:
parsley sprigs
strips of lemon rind

1 Place the asparagus, mushrooms, ginger and butter into a large frying pan and mix. Gently melt the butter and allow the vegetables to cook slowly, without browning, for about 5-8 minutes.

2 Add the tarragon and cream or crème fraîche to the pan, with salt and pepper to taste. Stir, then simmer for 5 minutes.

3 Bring at least 1.75 litres/3 pints water to the boil in a large saucepan. Add a dash of oil and a generous pinch of salt. Cook the pasta for 4-6 minutes or until it rises to the surface of the boiling water.

4 Drain the pasta and return it to the clean saucepan, pour the asparagus and mushroom sauce over and stir carefully. Garnish with parsley and strips of lemon rind.

Serves 4
Preparation time: 10 minutes
Cooking time: 20 minutes

Cappellini with Salsa

oil, see method

300 g/10 oz dried cappellini (angel hair pasta)

salt and pepper

1 tablespoon chopped fresh parsley, to garnish

SALSA:

1 onion, chopped finely

1 green pepper, cored, deseeded and diced

1 teaspoon hot chilli sauce

500 g/1 lb plum tomatoes, chopped

1 Make the salsa. Place the onion, pepper, chilli sauce and tomatoes in a bowl, mix well, then set aside for about 10 minutes.

2 Meanwhile, bring at least 1.75 litres/3 pints water to the boil in a large saucepan. Add a dash of oil and a generous pinch of salt. Cook the pasta for 5-7 minutes, until just tender.

3 Drain the pasta and return it to the clean pan. Add the salsa and toss well. Add salt and pepper to taste. Serve at once, garnished with the parsley.

Serves 4

Preparation time: 10 minutes, plus 10 minutes marinating time

Cooking time: 7 minutes

VARIATIONS

Grilled Cappellini Salsa

Cook the pasta and make the hot salsa as in the variation at right. Having tossed them together, transfer the mixture to a lightly greased 1.2 litre/2 pint ovenproof dish. Sprinkle over 125 g/4 oz grated mozzarella and grill for about 15 minutes or until the topping is golden.

Cappellini with Creamy Salsa

Make the salsa as in the main recipe, but instead of setting it aside for 10 minutes, transfer it to a small saucepan. Stir in 125 g/4 oz full fat soft cheese. Slowly bring to the boil over a moderate heat, stirring, then lower the heat and simmer for 3 minutes. Remove the pan from the heat. Cook the pasta as in the main recipe, return it to the pan in which it was cooked and add the sauce. Proceed as in the main recipe.

Spaghetti with Marinated Vegetables

1 red pepper, halved and deseeded
1 tablespoon salt
1 small aubergine, sliced
125 g/4 oz flat field mushrooms
1 leek, trimmed, cleaned and
   sliced thinly
1 teaspoon cumin seeds
½ teaspoon coriander seeds

150 ml/¼ pint raspberry vinegar
300 ml/½ pint olive oil
1 tablespoon garlic purée
salt and pepper
300 g/10 oz dried spaghetti
TO GARNISH
mixed salad leaves
flat leaf parsley

1 Place the red pepper on a grill pan, skin side up, and grill under a high heat for about 10 minutes until the skins have blackened and blistered. Remove from the heat and leave to cool.
2 Meanwhile, sprinkle the salt over the aubergine slices, set aside for 15 minutes. Drain the aubergine slices, rinse them well and pat dry with paper towels. Place the aubergine slices on a grill pan, and grill under a high heat for 10 minutes, turning the slices once, until browned. Remove from the grill pan.
3 Add the mushrooms to the grill pan and grill for 2 minutes.
4 Peel the peppers and finely slice the flesh. Slice the mushrooms. Combine the grilled vegetables in a large bowl and add the leek. Stir in the spices, vinegar, oil and garlic purée with salt and pepper to taste. Toss the mixture until well combined, and set aside.
5 Bring at least 1.75 litres/3 pints water to the boil in a large saucepan. Add a dash of oil and a generous pinch of salt. Cook the pasta for 8-12 minutes, until just tender. Drain thoroughly and add to the vegetable mixture. Toss again and chill for 3 hours before serving.
6 Serve garnished with salad leaves and flat leaf parsley.

Serves 4
Preparation time: 20 minutes
Cooking time: 20 minutes, plus 3 hours chilling time

Deep-fried Camembert with Fettuccine

8 Camembert wedges, chilled
2 eggs, beaten
125 g/4 oz fresh
   wholemeal breadcrumbs
1 teaspoon paprika
1 tablespoon chopped fresh parsley
oil for deep frying
300 g/10 oz fresh fettuccine pasta
1 tablespoon olive oil
1 tablespoon raspberry vinegar
salt and pepper

TO GARNISH:
fresh raspberries
raspberry leaves

1 Dip the Camembert wedges in egg, then in breadcrumbs to coat completely. Sprinkle with paprika and chill the wedges on a plate for 30 minutes.
2 Bring at least 1.75 litres/3 pints water to the boil in a large saucepan. Add a dash of oil and a generous pinch of salt. Cook the pasta for about 8-12 minutes, until just tender.
3 Heat the oil for deep frying to 180-190°C (350-375°F) – or until a cube of bread browns in 30 seconds. Fry the Camembert for 1 minute, turning once. Drain on paper towels and keep hot.
4 Drain the pasta and return to the clean saucepan. Add the oil and vinegar and season to taste. Toss well, twirl into 4 nests and place on heated serving plates. Add 2 deep-fried Camembert wedges to each portion. Garnish with raspberries and raspberry leaves and serve redcurrant jelly separately, if liked.

Serves 4
Preparation time: 10 minutes
Cooking time: 12 minutes

Field Mushroom Tortellini

Large field mushrooms seem to have a more 'mushroomy' taste than their cultivated cousins. They are quite widely available, but if you don't have any on hand, you could substitute ordinary button mushrooms, and add a few dried porcini, soaked in a little boiling water, to add extra zing to the taste.

oil, see method
300 g/10 oz dried tortellini
25 g/1 oz butter
500 g/1 lb field mushrooms,
    thinly sliced
3 shallots, chopped finely
2 tablespoons chopped fresh oregano
250 ml/8 fl oz double cream
salt and pepper
25 g/1 oz Parmesan cheese

1 Bring at least 1.75 litres/3 pints water to the boil in a large saucepan. Add a dash of oil and a generous pinch of salt. Cook the pasta for about 8-12 minutes, until just tender.
2 Meanwhile melt the butter in a large frying pan and fry the mushrooms and shallots for 5 minutes.
3 Reduce the heat and stir in the oregano and cream, with salt and pepper to taste. Simmer for about 5 minutes or until the cream has started to thicken.

4 Drain the pasta and return it to the clean saucepan. Stir in the cream sauce. Serve on heated plates with shavings of Parmesan cheese.

Serves 4
Preparation time: 10 minutes
Cooking time: 12 minutes

Pasta-packed Baked Red Peppers

4 red peppers, halved, cored
   and deseeded
125 g/4 oz mini macaroni, cooked
2 plum tomatoes, chopped
125 g/4 oz Cheddar cheese, grated
2 spring onions, chopped finely
2 tablespoons chopped fresh parsley
3 tablespoons olive oil
salt and pepper

1 Place the peppers on a baking sheet with the hollows uppermost. Mix the macaroni, tomatoes, cheese, spring onions and parsley in a bowl. Spoon into the peppers, drizzle with plenty of olive oil and add salt and pepper to taste.
2 Bake in a preheated oven, 180°C (350°F), Gas Mark 4, for 35-45 minutes or until the filling is golden and bubbling.
3 Serve at once, with fresh crusty bread.

Serves 4
Preparation time: 20 minutes
Cooking time: 45 minutes
Oven temperature: 180°C (350°F), Gas Mark 4

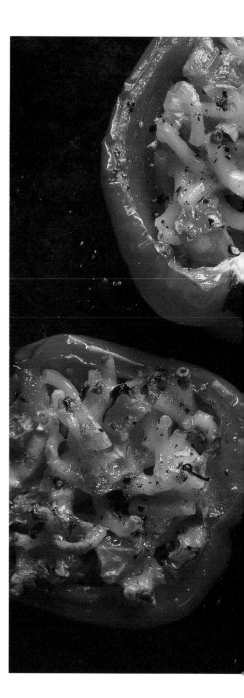

Balsamic Aubergine Salad

1 large aubergine, sliced
1 tablespoon salt
150 ml/¼ pint olive oil
300 g/10 oz dried penne rigate
6 tablespoons balsamic vinegar
1 teaspoon Dijon mustard
2 celery sticks, chopped
125 g/4 oz drained canned red kidney beans
salt and pepper
1 tablespoon chopped fresh parsley, to garnish

1 Spread out the aubergine slices on baking sheets and sprinkle with the salt. Set aside for 15 minutes.

2 Meanwhile, bring at least 1.75 litres/3 pints water to the boil in a large saucepan. Add a dash of oil and a generous pinch of salt. Cook the pasta for 8-12 minutes, until just tender.

3 Drain the pasta and rinse under cold water in a colander. Drain again, transfer to a large salad bowl and set aside.

4 Rinse the aubergines slices under plenty of cold water, drain and pat dry with paper towels. Grill under a high heat for 10 minutes until crisp, turning once. Slice each aubergine round in half. Set aside.

5 In a bowl, whisk the olive oil with the vinegar and Dijon mustard. Add salt and pepper to taste. Add the dressing to the pasta and toss well. Fold in the celery and kidney beans, with the reserved aubergine slices. Scatter the parsley on top and serve at once.

Serves 4
Preparation time: 20 minutes, plus 15 minutes standing time
Cooking time: 12 minutes

Asparagus and Parma Ham Salad

Condiverdi or antipasto mixes are delicious combinations of vegetables marinated in a seasoned dressing and sold in 290 g/9½ oz jars. Sliced mushrooms may be substituted if condiverdi is unavailable.

300 g/10 oz dried laganele or farfalle
75 g/3 oz Parma ham, cut into strips
250 g/8 oz asparagus spears, cooked
   and chopped
6 tablespoons condiverdi
salt and pepper
25 g/1 oz fresh Parmesan cheese
salt and pepper
1 tablespoon chopped fresh parsley,
   to garnish

1 Bring at least 1.75 litres/3 pints water to the boil. Add a dash of oil and a pinch of salt. Cook the pasta for 8-12 minutes, until just tender.
2 Drain the pasta, rinse it under cold water in a colander then transfer to a large salad bowl.
3 Add the Parma ham, asparagus and condiverdi; toss well. Add salt and pepper to taste. Using a potato peeler, pare the Parmesan into long shavings. Carefully fold into the pasta. Serve, garnished with parsley.

Serves 4
Preparation time: 10 minutes
Cooking time: 12 minutes

Lumaconi and Smoked Mackerel Salad

'Lumaconi' means 'big snails', and this pasta does look like snails' shells. Any large shell-shaped pasta may be used instead, and smaller ones would probably be preferable in the variation at right.

300 g/10 oz dried lumaconi
2 fillets peppered smoked mackerel, skinned and broken into bite-sized pieces
2 oranges, segmented
½ cucumber, chopped
sprigs of fresh dill, to garnish
DRESSING:
1-2 tablespoons wholegrain mustard
3 tablespoons orange juice
1 teaspoon lemon juice
3 tablespoons olive oil
salt and pepper

1 Bring at least 1.75 litres/3 pints water to the boil in a large saucepan. Add a dash of oil and a generous pinch of salt. Cook the pasta for 8-12 minutes.
2 Drain the pasta and rinse under cold running water in a colander. Drain again, transfer to a large salad bowl and add the mackerel. Mix lightly.
3 Make the dressing. Place the mustard, orange juice, lemon juice and oil in a screw-top jar. Close the jar tightly and shake well. Add salt and pepper, shake the dressing again and pour over the salad.
4 Finish the salad by folding in the orange segments and cucumber. Garnish with sprigs of dill.

Serves 4
Preparation time: 20 minutes
Cooking time: 12 minutes

VARIATION
Shellfish Cocktail

Cook the pasta as in the main recipe and instead of the mackerel, add 3 rollmop herrings, finely sliced, and 50 g/2 oz each of peeled cooked prawns and drained bottled cockles in vinegar. Toss in a dressing of 1 tablespoon tomato purée, 4 tablespoons light mayonnaise, 1 teaspoon mild chilli powder and 2 teaspoons lemon juice. Spoon over Iceberg lettuce leaves in 4 individual glass bowls.

Three-bean Pasta Twist Salad

oil, see method
300 g/10 oz dried tricolore
   pasta twists
2 spring onions, chopped diagonally
1 red pepper, cored, deseeded
   and chopped
125 g/4 oz drained canned red
   kidney beans

125 g/4 oz drained canned
   pinto beans
125 g/4 oz drained canned
   borlotti beans
200 ml/7 fl oz crème fraîche
4 tablespoons milk
3 tablespoons chopped fresh dill
salt and pepper

1 Bring at least 1.75 litres/3 pints water to the boil in a large saucepan. Add a dash of oil and a generous pinch of salt. Cook the pasta for 8-12 minutes, until just tender. Drain the pasta, rinse under cold water in a colander, drain again and transfer to a large salad bowl.

2 Add the spring onions, red pepper and beans. Mix well. Beat the crème fraîche and milk together in a bowl; fold into the salad and add salt and freshly ground black pepper to taste.

3 Fold in the dill and serve.

Serves 4
Preparation time: 20 minutes
Cooking time: 12 minutes

Winter Macaroni Salad

When using wholemeal pasta always allow a little more cooking time as it takes longer to absorb water. However, for this particular recipe, check the pasta after 10 minutes. If it has a bite to it when tasted, drain and use at once. Do not overcook the pasta as there is quite a lot of additional sauce.

oil, see method
300 g/10 oz dried
   wholemeal macaroni
¼ white cabbage, shredded
1 onion, sliced into rings
2 carrots, cut into thin sticks
1 leek, trimmed, cleaned and
   sliced finely
250 g/8 oz rindless back bacon,
   grilled and chopped
6 tablespoons light mayonnaise
4 tablespoons milk
2 tablespoons tomato purée
salt and pepper
1 tablespoon chopped fresh parsley,
   to garnish

1 Bring at least 1.75 litres/3 pints water to the boil in a large saucepan. Add a dash of oil and a pinch of salt. Cook the pasta for about 8-12 minutes, until just tender.
2 Drain the pasta under cold water in a colander, drain again and transfer to a large salad bowl.

3 Add the cabbage, onion, carrots, leek and half the bacon to the salad bowl. Toss well with the pasta and add salt and pepper to taste.
4 Mix the mayonnaise and milk, with the tomato purée in a bowl. Spoon into the salad and toss well.

Garnish with the chopped parsley and chill until required.

Serves 4
Preparation time: 20 minutes
Cooking time: 12 minutes

Chinese Duck Salad

This warm salad has a delicious Chinese flavour, thanks to the hoisin-flavoured duck.

oil, see method
250 g/8 oz dried vermicelli
250 g/8 oz duck breast
6 tablespoons hoisin sauce
3 spring onions, sliced diagonally
2.5 cm/1 inch piece of fresh root
    ginger, grated
½ head Chinese leaf salad, shredded
2 tomatoes, sliced
1 carrot, grated
125 g/4 oz broccoli florets, cooked
125 g/4 oz baby sweetcorn, cooked
    and halved

1 Bring at least 1.75 litres/3 pints water to the boil in a large saucepan. Add a dash of oil and a generous pinch of salt. Add the pasta, remove from the heat, cover the pan and leave it to stand for about 6 minutes.
2 Meanwhile brush the duck breast generously with the hoisin sauce. Grill under high heat for 20 minutes, turning once.
3 Meanwhile, drain the pasta and rinse under cold water in a colander. Drain again, transfer to a large salad bowl, add a little oil and toss well to separate any sticky strands. Add all the remaining ingredients and toss well.

4 Remove the duck from the grill, cool for 5 minutes and slice thinly. Add to the salad and toss lightly.

Serves 4-6
Preparation time: 30 minutes
Cooking time: 30 minutes

Chicken and Mushroom Penne Salad

300 g/10 oz fresh penne or dried
   wholemeal penne
250 g/8 oz cooked chicken breast,
   sliced into strips
125 g/4 oz button mushrooms, sliced
1 red pepper, halved, cored, deseeded
   and sliced finely

3 tablespoons sesame oil
1 teaspoon sesame seeds
1 tablespoon lemon juice
4 spring onions, sliced diagonally
salt and pepper
2 tablespoons chopped fresh parsley,
   to garnish

1 Bring at least 1.75 litres/3 pints water to the boil in a large saucepan. Add a dash of oil and a generous pinch of salt. Cook fresh pasta for 4-8 minutes; dried pasta for 8-12 minutes. Drain the pasta, rinse under cold water in a colander and drain again. Transfer to a large salad bowl.

2 Add the chicken, mushrooms and red pepper, with the oil, sesame seeds, lemon juice and spring onions. Add salt and pepper to taste and toss well. Garnish with the chopped parsley.

Serves 4
Preparation time: 30 minutes
Cooking time: 8-12 minutes

VARIATIONS

Chicken Salad with Avocado and Raspberry Vinegar

Make the salad as for the main recipe omitting the lemon juice. Toss 1 sliced avocado in 2 tablespoons raspberry vinegar. Season with plenty of black pepper. Add the avocado to the salad with 2 chopped plum tomatoes, or heap the salad on a large platter and arrange the avocado with plum tomato slices around the rim. Sprinkle a little chopped basil over the tomato.

Spanish Sausage and Chicken

Cook the pasta as for the main recipe. Add the chicken and mushrooms but not the red peppers. Slice 2 chorizo sausages and add them to the salad with 1 sliced, deseeded, green pepper. Omit the sesame oil and sesame seeds from the dressing; instead, whisk 2 tablespoons mild chilli sauce with the lemon juice and spring onions. Add salt and pepper to taste and toss well. Garnish with the chopped parsley as for the main recipe.

Tuna Pasta Shell Salad

One of the very best pasta salads – equally good with cooked fresh tuna, especially if it has been barbecued. The combination of tuna, walnuts and pesto also makes a very good sauce with hot pasta too.

4 tablespoons olive oil
400 g/13 oz fresh pasta shells
5 tablespoons ready-made pesto
1 teaspoon white wine vinegar
1 teaspoon grated lemon rind
1 x 200 g/7 oz can tuna in brine,
   drained and flaked
50 g/2 oz walnut pieces
salt and pepper
6 large basil leaves, shredded

1 Bring at least 1.75 litres/3 pints water to the boil in a large saucepan. Add a dash of oil and a generous pinch of salt. Cook the pasta shells for about 4-8 minutes, or until it rises to the surface of the boiling water.
2 Drain the pasta, rinse under cold running water in a colander and drain again. Transfer to a large salad bowl.
3 Mix the pesto sauce and vinegar in a bowl. Season well with black pepper. Add to the pasta with the grated lemon rind and toss well.
4 Fold the tuna and walnuts into the pasta. Sprinkle with the basil and

drizzle the olive oil over the top. Mix carefully, then serve immediately, or chill until required.

Serves 4
Preparation time: 10 minutes
Cooking time: 8 minutes

Herb Sausage and Garlic Penne Salad

250 g/8 oz herb pork sausages
4 tablespoons light olive oil
300 g/10 oz dried penne
1-2 garlic cloves, crushed
1 shallot, chopped finely
2 gherkins, chopped finely
1 tablespoon chopped fresh parsley
salt and pepper
1 teaspoon chopped fresh parsley,
   to garnish

1 Grill the sausages until cooked right through and crisp on the outside. Remove from the heat and cool for 10 minutes.

2 Bring at least 1.75 litres/3 pints water to the boil in a large saucepan. Add a dash of oil and a pinch of salt. Cook the pasta for 8-12 minutes, until just tender.

3 Drain the pasta, rinse under cold water in a colander and drain again. Transfer to a large salad bowl. Mix the garlic, shallot, gherkins, remaining oil and parsley in a bowl. Add to the pasta with salt and pepper to taste; toss well.

4 Cut the sausages into large chunks and stir them into the salad. Garnish with the chopped parsley. Serve or chill until required.

Serves 4
Preparation time: 10 minutes
Cooking time: 25-35 minutes

Warm Italian Mix Salad

300 g/10 oz dried pasta wheels
1 red pepper, cored, deseeded
   and quartered
125 g/4 oz mozzarella cheese, grated
125 g/4 oz Red Leicester
   cheese, grated
50 g/2 oz salami slices, chopped

2 ripe plum tomatoes, chopped
50 g/2 oz stoned black olives
2 tablespoons lemon juice
salt and pepper
1 tablespoon chopped fresh parsley,
   to garnish

1 Bring at least 1.75 litres/3 pints water to the boil in a large saucepan. Add a dash of oil and a generous pinch of salt. Cook the pasta for 8-12 minutes, until just tender.

2 Meanwhile, place the red pepper in a grill pan, skin side uppermost. Grill under a high heat until the skins have blackened and blistered. Remove the pepper quarters from the heat and set aside to cool for 5 minutes.

3 Drain the pasta in a colander and toss immediately with the grated cheeses. Transfer to a large salad bowl.

4 Peel away the pepper skin. Slice the flesh and add to the pasta with the salami, tomatoes and black olives.

5 Add the lemon juice, with salt and pepper to taste; toss well. Garnish with parsley and serve immediately, while still warm.

Serves 4
Preparation time: 20 minutes
Cooking time: 12 minutes

Goats' Cheese and Watercress Conchiglie

6 tablespoons olive oil
300 g/10 oz dried conchiglie
3 spring onions, sliced diagonally
3 tablespoons raspberry vinegar
salt and pepper
125 g/4 oz soft goats' cheese, diced
1 orange or grapefruit, segmented
1 bunch watercress, washed
    and trimmed

1 Bring 1.75 litres/3 pints water to the boil in a large saucepan. Add a dash of oil and a generous pinch of salt. Cook the pasta for about 8-12 minutes, until just tender.
2 Drain the pasta, rinse under cold running water in a colander and drain again. Transfer to a large salad bowl.
3 Mix the spring onions, vinegar and remaining oil in a bowl. Add salt and pepper to taste and pour over the pasta.
4 Fold in the goats' cheese, the orange or grapefruit segments and watercress. Toss and chill until required.

Serves 4
Preparation time: 10 minutes
Cooking time: 12 minutes

Broccoli and Red Pepper Fettuccine

6 tablespoons olive oil
300 g/10 oz fresh fettuccine
3 red peppers, deseeded and halved
250 g/8 oz small broccoli florets
2 tablespoons balsamic vinegar
salt and pepper
basil leaves, to garnish

1 Bring at least 1.75 litres/3 pints water to the boil in a large saucepan. Add a dash of oil and a pinch of salt. Cook the pasta for 4-6 minutes, until just tender.
2 Drain, rinse under cold water in a colander and drain again. Set aside in a large salad bowl.
3 Grill the peppers, skin side up, until the skins have blackened and blistered. Remove from the heat and leave to cool for 5 minutes.
4 Meanwhile, bring a saucepan of lightly salted water to the boil in a large saucepan and blanch the broccoli for 3 minutes. Drain, rinse under cold water and drain again.
5 Peel the peppers and slice the flesh into strips. Add to the pasta with the drained broccoli florets, remaining olive oil and balsamic vinegar. Add salt and pepper to taste and toss well. Serve at once, garnished with basil leaves.

Serves 4
Preparation time: 10 minutes
Cooking time: about 15 minutes

VARIATIONS

Chickpea, Spinach and Mushroom Fettuccine

Make the salad as for the main recipe, omitting the broccoli. Substitute 125 g/4 oz drained canned chickpeas, 25 g/1 oz torn young spinach leaves and 25 g/1 oz sliced mushrooms. Add the dressing, toss well, then serve with a little soured cream.

Fettuccine Verdi with Gorgonzola

Substitute green fettuccine for the plain pasta in the main recipe. Cook, drain, rinse under cold running water, drain again, and transfer to a salad bowl. Add the red peppers but omit the broccoli when mixing the salad; stir in 250 g/8 oz cubed Gorgonzola cheese and about 25 g/1 oz toasted pine nuts. Use white wine vinegar instead of balsamic vinegar in the salad dressing and add 1 teaspoon Dijon mustard.

Artichoke and Pesto Salad

2 tablespoons olive oil
300 g/10 oz dried mista tricolore
(tomato, spinach and plain pasta)
1 x 397 g/14 oz can artichoke hearts,
drained and quartered
4 tablespoons ready-made pesto

4 anchovies, chopped
2 teaspoons capers, chopped
50 g/2 oz Parmesan cheese, grated
salt and pepper
red onion rings, to garnish

1 Bring at least 1.75 litres/3 pints water to the boil in a large saucepan. Add a dash of oil and a generous pinch of salt. Cook the pasta for 8-12 minutes, until just tender.

2 Drain the pasta, rinse under cold running water in a colander, drain again, then set aside.

3 Place the artichoke hearts in a large salad bowl with the pesto, remaining olive oil, anchovies, capers and Parmesan cheese. Stir well; season with pepper.

4 Add the pasta to the bowl and toss well, adding a little more olive oil if necessary. Garnish with the onion rings.

Serves 4
Preparation time: 10 minutes
Cooking time: 12 minutes

Greek Tarragon Salad

6 tablespoons olive oil
300 g/10 oz dried egg tronchetti
250 g/8 oz feta cheese, diced
1 red onion, sliced thinly
10 black olives, stoned and halved
2 plum tomatoes, chopped
1 bunch fresh tarragon
2 tablespoons tarragon vinegar
salt and pepper

1 Bring at least 1.75 litres/3 pints water to the boil in a large saucepan. Add a dash of oil and a pinch of salt. Cook the pasta for about 8-12 minutes, until just tender.
2 Drain the pasta, rinse under cold water in a colander, drain again then set aside.
3 Place the cheese and pasta in a large salad bowl. Add the onion rings, olives and tomatoes and toss well. Set aside a couple of sprigs of tarragon for the garnish. Strip the tarragon leaves from the remaining stems and add them to the salad with the pasta. Add salt and freshly ground black pepper to taste. Toss well and garnish with the reserved tarragon. Chill until required.

Serves 4
Preparation time: 10 minutes
Cooking time: 12 minutes

Mexican Pasta Salad

oil, see method
300 g/10 oz dried conchigliette rigate
2 ripe avocados
8 tablespoons soured cream
3 teaspoons chilli sauce
2 tablespoons lime juice
250 g/8 oz red kidney beans, drained
salt and pepper
cayenne pepper, to garnish

1 Bring at least 1.75 litres/3 pints water to the boil in a large saucepan. Add a dash of oil and a generous pinch of salt. Cook the pasta for about 8-12 minutes, until just tender.
2 Drain the pasta, rinse under cold running water in a colander, drain again and then transfer to a large salad bowl.
3 Halve the avocados and remove the stones. Put the flesh in a food processor or bowl. Add the soured cream, chilli sauce and lime juice. Process for 1 minute. Alternatively, mash the avocado with a fork and stir in the remaining ingredients.
4 Spoon the sauce over the pasta and stir well. Add salt and pepper to taste. Add the kidney beans, toss well and serve, sprinkled with cayenne pepper.

Serves 4
Preparation time: 10 minutes
Cooking time: 12 minutes